The Kitchen  Planner

The Kitchen Planner

Hundreds of Great Ideas for Your New Kitchen

CHRONICLE BOOKS

SAN FRANCISCO

THE KITCHEN PLANNER Suzanne Ardley

First published in the United States in 1999 by Chronicle Books LLC
First published in the United Kingdom in 1999
by Mitchell Beazley, an imprint of Octopus Publishing Group Ltd
2-4 Heron Quays, Docklands, London. E14 4JP
www.mitchell-beazley.co.uk

Typeset in Avenir and Helvetica
Produced by Toppan Printing Co (HK) Ltd
Reproduction by Colourpath and Erayscan Pte. Ltd
Printed and bound in China

Executive Editor Judith More
Editor Claire Musters
Executive Art Editor Janis Utton
Production Karen Farquhar

Produced for Mitchell Beazley by Walton and Pringle
www.waltonandpringle.com
Project Editor Bella Pringle
Consultant Suzanne Ardley
Art Editor Colin Walton
Picture Research Alexandra Myers

Cover design Laura Lovett
Cover photographs David Duncan Livingston
www.davidduncanlivingston.com

Library of Congress Cataloging-in-Publication Data available.

ISBN: 0-8118-2517-5

Distributed in Canada by Raincoast Books
9050 Shaughnessy Street
Vancouver BC V6P 6E5

10 9 8 7 6 5 4

Chronicle Books LLC
85 Second Street
San Francisco, CA 94105
www.chroniclebooks.com

CONTENTS

Introduction

A new kitchen is often the second most expensive purchase after the house itself, so take time to plan it well. The purpose of this book is to help formulate your ideas into a successful, practical design that will match your individual needs and lifestyle.

1 A large range with choice of ovens, burners, griddle, and warming plates is ideal for cooking on a grand scale. The stainless-steel backsplash is easy to clean, and a hanging rack keeps utensils within easy reach.

2 Natural wood finishes have a warm, restful appearance and the advantage of wearing well and mellowing with age. Glass brick walls and opaque glass cabinet doors maintain a light, airy atmosphere.

Kitchens are busy places with much activity gravitating in and around them. For many, the kitchen serves several purposes, and it is frequently the most used room in the home. A new kitchen must be planned to meet your specific needs, so before you begin, consider the various demands of those who will use it. The choices of singles or career couples are likely to differ from those of a family with children and pets. If a member of the family has a physical limitation, their needs have to be taken into account too. Casual entertaining at the kitchen table, where the sounds and smells provide a friendly, relaxed atmosphere for guests, may be a priority. Hobbies and homework also frequently take place in kitchens, enabling parents to cook at the same time as supervising children in a safe environment. If space permits, a couch or armchair may provide a "soft area" for play or watching television. If pets share your home, you will need an area where they can eat that is out of the way and will not obstruct access to equipment or storage.

3 This freestanding workbench provides a useful food preparation area with drawers beneath to hold utensils and knives. Open-sided shelving allows easy access and good visibility, and the surfaces are smooth and easily cleaned.

How suitable is your room?

The quickest and simplest option is to remodel an existing kitchen. However, often the shape is restrictive, and architectural features such as windows, doors, or steps are badly positioned for the ideas you have in mind. Look carefully at the room to assess how it functions with others in the home. Do you have to pass through other rooms or walk up and down steps with heavy groceries to reach the present kitchen? Is the kitchen separated from the eating area, necessitating walks between the two and inefficient use of the space between? Is there sufficient floor area within the room for all the standard appliances and cabinets you wish to incorporate? Before embarking on remodeling an existing kitchen, consider various other options: an adjacent room may provide the ideal solution; as an alternative, knocking through an adjoining wall to make one large kitchen room may present a host of new and exciting options.

What could you change?

Start by noting any problems you encounter regularly in the existing kitchen that could be improved or

PLAN OF ACTION

Once you have established your budget, calculate how much needs to be spent on building alterations as well as the services of an electrician, plumber, and carpenter, and refer to the list below:

☑ Will you need the help of a professional, such as an architect, for planning structural alterations?

☑ Have the relevant authorities given you permission for your proposed structural alterations?

☑ Can you do any of the preparation work yourself, such as remove old cabinets and fittings?

☑ Do you have quotes from the various contractors, to make sure that costs do not escalate?

☑ Have you made plans to use another room for eating, cooking, and storage while work is in progress?

☑ Does your budget allow for decoration of the new kitchen, including items such as window shades?

cross refer to
activity areas 54
selecting equipment 70
kitchen materials 84
quick-fix changes 98

key to icons
appliances
flooring
furniture
lighting
planning
utilities
storage
surfaces
windows

4 Combining a place to work and a place to relax allows different family members to work and play at the same time. Here, the couch provides a natural break between the cooking and "soft" living area of the room.

5 Pull-out shelving and drawers make the storage of equipment considerably easier and efficient. Sections in the angled drawer are designed to hold sharp items securely in place.

6 Quick snacks and drinks are simple to make and eat at this combined preparation and breakfast bar.

4

replaced. In addition to the cabinets, countertops, flooring, and general color scheme, look at less obvious details: does the window provide enough natural daylight, and is the artificial lighting adaptable enough? Is the sink large enough, and is it comfortable to stand at for long periods? Are there sufficient electrical and plumbing outlets? Could repositioning items such as the heater or window free up enough wall space to create an alternative kitchen layout?

All kitchen fittings and equipment need to be functional and easily maintained. The following pages look in detail at the options available – cabinets, fittings, surfaces, and appliances – to help you choose the designs that will suit you best.

Maximizing efficiency

Space is a key element when planning any kitchen, and maximizing the efficiency of the room – whatever its size – will make it a pleasure to use. Consider the main functions of preparing and cooking food, as well as the other activities that take place in the kitchen: look at how these main activity areas operate in relation to others in the room, and how the space can be organized to link a range of activities successfully. To achieve a good work flow, think about the time spent moving between each activity area and plan how to avoid cramped areas or long walks around widely spaced zones.

5

6

Assessing your space: singles

Determine how often you cook at home and how often you entertain, and match your kitchen plan to your lifestyle needs.

 ONE-WALL GALLEY

 TWO-WALL GALLEY

If you often eat out or come home late from work, plan a kitchen equipped with time-saving appliances. If you often entertain, arrange the room accordingly.

▤ If you live on your own but enjoy cooking with plenty of fresh ingredients, plan a full-height refrigerator at the end of the cabinet run for chilled storage, and allow plenty of counter space for food preparation.

▨ For those in small apartments where the kitchen and living area occupy one room, decide whether it is important to be able to screen off the kitchen, or whether you would like it to remain open so that you can talk to your guests while cooking.

▨ If you entertain frequently, provide an area for friends to sit in the kitchen so that you do not have to work alone. A pass-through between the kitchen and dining area will also cut down on trips between rooms.

▤ Those living alone will probably need less cabinet space for storing non-perishable foods and a large fridge-freezer for ready-prepared meals and leftovers. To make a narrow two-wall galley feel more spacious, consider doing away with wall cabinets.

To make the kitchen more efficient, decide which activities you perform most frequently and give them priority when positioning major items.

◩ For safety and convenience, make sure that the countertops are well lit by positioning the lights in front of where you work so that you do not cast a shadow. If the kitchen is part of the living room, install dimmers so that the lights can be softened when you are entertaining guests.

▤ If you live on your own it is tempting to leave clutter on countertops, but keeping surfaces clear makes it easier to work in the limited space of a galley kitchen.

▨ Even those people working alone in a two-wall galley kitchen should allow room for doors on appliances and cabinets to open fully. Make sure that you can bend down to look inside without touching the cabinets on the opposite wall.

▦ If you tend to cook quick and easy meals for one on the cooktop, such as stir-fries, try to place the cooktop along an exterior wall so that the ventilation hood can be installed with the minimum amount of ducting.

When the kitchen layout is resolved, plan the order in which electrical and plumbing work, cabinet installation, and floor or tile laying should be carried out.

◩ Water and power will be unavailable while work is carried out, and kitchen equipment will need to be stored elsewhere. If you live in a small studio apartment, arrange for work to take place while you are on vacation or staying with friends.

▨ Before the plumbing work is done, consider whether you should include a dishwasher in your plan – compact versions are available and practical for small kitchens, as they occupy very little space.

◩ Before you install a two-wall galley kitchen, make sure that the electrician fits wires along the length of both preparation counters. Even for one it is important to have a choice of work areas with adequate lighting.

◆ The kitchen floor should be laid before base cabinets are installed and then protected when they are fitted. For those who live on their own, inevitably there will be less kitchen traffic, giving individual taste priority over practical considerations, such as durability.

KEY

- ⚡ planning
- 🔥 utilities
- 🗄 storage
- ▦ appliances
- 🍳 small appliances
- 🪑 furniture
- ▪ surfaces
- ✦ flooring
- ▦ windows
- 💡 lighting

 L-SHAPE

 U-SHAPE

 ISLAND

L-SHAPE

▦ A full-size dishwasher is worth considering if you live alone, especially if you enjoy entertaining large groups of people. An L-shaped kitchen has plenty of below-counter space for this extra appliance. Install it close to the sink so that it can be easily plumbed in.

▦ Plan a counter area for a microwave so that you can heat up ready-made meals for one. Consider a combination microwave and oven which will take up the same amount of space as a regular microwave.

💡 Singles can plan the kitchen lighting perfectly to suit their own height so that they do not cast shadows over the area they are working in and the lights do not cause glare as they move from one area to the next.

🪑 If you are a sociable single or work from home, plan an area in the kitchen for a telephone and notepad or diary so that while you are busy in the kitchen, you can take calls and jot down any engagements while keeping a watchful eye on your cooking.

✦ When deciding on your flooring needs, consider a soft rug with an anti-slip backing to cover the hard floor in the eating/relaxing area of the L-shaped kitchen. This will provide a comfortable surface to walk across barefoot or stretch out on to read a book or watch television when you are alone.

🪑 It is best to wait until the kitchen is installed before buying any furniture – as a single person you have the flexibility to choose the size of table to suit the room shape.

U-SHAPE

▦ A microwave and hot water dispenser may be the only items used regularly in a singles' kitchen. However, in a U-shaped kitchen you will have enough counter space to include occasional small appliances such as a blender, coffee grinder, and toaster.

▦ When you live alone, it does not matter if appliances take up counter space. When guests offer to help, create more space with a chopping block that fits over the sink so that they have more counter space.

🔥 For ease of plumbing, sinks are often placed against an exterior wall, and directly below a window. If the view from the window is good, consider placing a breakfast bar here instead of a sink so that meals alone take on an interesting new aspect.

▪ Those singles who do not have a kitchen table, should plan a clear space for unpacking shopping and grocery bags. Allow at least one unbroken stretch of countertop to prepare food as well.

🔥 For singles on a tight budget, but with space for a U-shaped kitchen, the extra cost of complicated plumbing runs around corners can be avoided by arranging the sink, faucets, hot water dispenser, and dishwasher along one wall.

🔥 If you live alone in a studio apartment and the U-shaped kitchen has windows on two sides, consider fitting underfloor heating when plumbing work is carried out, rather than wall-mounted radiators which take up space.

ISLAND

⚡ Island kitchens are practical for those who have a large room. For those who live alone, islands help focus activities in one area and save time spent moving across the room.

▦ A cooktop placed in the center of the kitchen enables the lone cook to face the room when at work rather than a wall.

▦ A hanging rack above the island will keep pots and pans and other kitchen utensils within easy reach of the solitary cook.

🪑 Plan an off-set or movable island on wheels to allow space for a dining table in the kitchen if you entertain regularly.

🔥 If you live alone, make sure that you know how to switch off water, electricity, and gas on the island, and that it is easy to access these utilities for repair.

▦ Install a ventilator hood above the island that is powerful enough to remove odors from the stove when cooking.

🪑 Freestanding island designs that have a chopping block and storage area but no cooking or washing facilities, are ideal for singles who frequently move as they can be taken from home to home.

✦ Plumbing and electrical connections for a sink and stovetop on an island will need to run under the floor. The kitchen will be out of action so plan meals out with family or friends or, if you work from home, make other arrangements for a few days.

Assessing your space: couples

Career couples may favor a low-maintenance kitchen filled with work-saving devices, which has enough space to entertain comfortably.

 ONE-WALL GALLEY

 TWO-WALL GALLEY

Consider how often both partners cook together and look at the style of food you enjoy cooking. Ask if you prefer formal or relaxed dinners.

- The paths of two people cooking in a one-wall galley kitchen will inevitably cross. Consider a movable butcher's block that can be used away from the fixed counters.

- Bear in mind that different-height partners may prefer to work at different-height counter levels for food preparation.

- If you intend to eat together in the kitchen, choose a pull-out table and folding chairs that allow both partners to sit in comfort but can be stored out of sight when not in use.

- Two people cooking at once in a two-wall galley is easier because one can concentrate on preparing ingredients on one side while the other uses the stovetop and oven on the other side of the kitchen.

- Avoid crossing the other user's path or standing back to back in a two-wall galley by making sure that the utensils needed for food preparation are housed next to the appropriate appliance and that the arrangement of appliances is staggered.

Two people sharing a kitchen may each have different methods of working. Compile a list of individual preferences and try to keep a flexible design.

- Make sure that there are enough electrical outlets for both partners to use food preparation appliances simultaneously.

- A sink with an extra half bowl makes good planning sense as it can be used by one person for washing ingredients without monopolizing the main sink.

- Plan an eye-level microwave in an appliance stack which is easy to reach by both partners and leaves the counter free.

- A pull-out table that can be locked into position for meals and food preparation is practical in a two-wall galley kitchen. Look for a design that can slide back into a recess between the base cabinets when not in use.

- When two people use the two-wall galley kitchen at the same time, consider fitting a double sink. This way, each of the sink bowls can be used independently by both people for washing vegetables and fruit, cleaning dishes, or rinsing pans.

Carefully organize and plan the remodeling schedule for the kitchen and be sure to calculate an accurate budget for the cost of labor and materials.

- If you have planned an eating area at countertop level, wait for the surface to be installed before looking for stools to make sure that they are a comfortable height for both of you to sit at without feeling cramped.

- Choose a window treatment, such as simple shades or shutters, that is easy to open and close by either partner. This way, shade or full sunlight can be selected without having to stretch or climb up to reach the mechanism, which can be unsafe to do in a kitchen.

- Fit wood, stone, and tile flooring before you install the cabinets as their thickness can obstruct the toe-kick and may not fit snugly into uneven areas. In addition, by placing the flooring under the cabinets, the countertop level can be adjusted to a level that is comfortable for both partners.

- If there is one main door leading to and from the kitchen, a small window in the door will help prevent accidents by allowing people on both sides to see if someone is in the way.

KEY

⬓ planning   ⬧ utilities   ▤ storage   ⊞ appliances   ⬧ small appliances

⬚ furniture   ▦ surfaces   ⬥ flooring   ⊡ windows   ⬩ lighting

 L-SHAPE

 U-SHAPE

 ISLAND

L-SHAPE	U-SHAPE	ISLAND
⬚ L-shaped kitchens are ideal for adding a dining area or relaxation area. If you want your partner to join in with the cooking they can; if not, they can still converse from a comfortable distance.	▤ Make sure that both partners can reach and remove heavier items stored in cabinets in the deep corners of U-shaped kitchens. Aim to store steps in a tall cabinet for smaller partners to reach high shelving.	⬓ Decide whether you want the island to function as a food preparation center or if you intend to cook or dine there. Organize storage for tableware, glasses, and flatware near the island to avoid interrupting the cook's movement.
▦ L-shaped kitches have plenty of free countertop space between appliances, especially in the corners. For busy career couples, consider low-maintenance finishes for counters so that you can spend less of your spare time cleaning.	⊞ If you or your partner like to be entertained when working in the kitchen, plan a wall-mounted site for television or audio equipment. Alternatively, the deep corners of U-shaped kitchens make the perfect location for a countertop television.	⊞ If a dishwasher or trash compactor is to be built into the island, choose a model with a low noise level and good sound insulation so meals and conversation will not be disrupted.

▤ If you and your partner like to keep a selection of wines in the kitchen, create a rack at the end of a run of base cabinets in the awkward space that sometimes cannot be avoided in L-shaped kitchen planning.	⬓ If no dining area exists outside of the U-shape, attach a folding table to the open wall to seat two to four people.	⬧ A low-level counter on the island with built-in electrical outlets set close by makes it possible for one partner to use blenders, grinders, and food processors in one specifically designed area. Plan a space beneath the low-level island counter so that items can be stored away.
⬧ If you or your partner want to be able to hear each other over the sound of appliances when working in the large floor area of an L-shaped kitchen, choose "soft" flooring materials, such as linoleum and select low-decibel appliances.	⬧ A hot water dispenser is invaluable if either partner works from home as it reduces fuel consumption and is a time-saver; it also keeps counter space free of a kettle.	▦ As several activities are often combined on an island in a shared home, make sure that your choice of surface can withstand heat, spills, and splashes.
	⬥ When both partners work, reduce the maintenance of large U-shaped rooms with easy-wipe cabinets and hardwearing floors.	

⬓ Fitting a large L-shaped kitchen can be quite an upheaval. If both partners work and one has to take time off to supervise the electricians, plumbers, and carpenters, set a completion date with the contractors so that you know, from the outset, how long it will take.	⬧ In a U-shaped kitchen there is only a small area of wall on show – the backsplash area and space between the top of the wall cabinets and ceiling. If you and your partner want to create an impression of light and airiness, paint the wall area in a pale color.	⬧ Remember that good ventilation will make the island and surrounding room comfortable for both partners. Down-draft systems on islands can be problematic to vent successfully. An overhead hood requires venting to an outside wall and needs installing before any other features.
⬩ Once the table is in place, select a light fitting that can provide subtle lighting for meals or a brighter beam of light for a person working at the table. A rise-and-fall pendant on a dimmer is easy to install.	⬚ If the door opens into a small U-shaped kitchen, reverse the hinges so that when one partner enters the kitchen they do not open the door onto the other person working at the counter or using appliances.	⬩ In large island kitchens, organize two-way lighting switches at both the door and island so that either partner, wherever they are in the room, can control the lighting.

Assessing your space: families

An efficient and safe family kitchen needs careful planning as it will be used for leisure activities as well as cooking and eating.

 ONE-WALL GALLEY

 TWO-WALL GALLEY

As the center of family life, the kitchen is often multifunctional with uses ranging from food preparation and eating to hobby and homework activities.

One-wall galleys do not have the space for a permanent table. Consider the needs of young children requiring supervised meals or older children who prefer to make their own quick snacks. A pull-out table is useful if sited away from hot surfaces.

Families produce large quantities of waste, which takes up valuable space in a small kitchen. Compost organic waste for use in the garden, or use a trash compactor to reduce the volume to a manageable level.

Two-wall galley kitchens offer more storage space than one-wall galleys. A tall pantry with a high shelf to store dangerous cleaning supplies out of reach is a good idea for families with small children.

Keep the dishwasher, garbage disposal, and trash can within one run so that family members clearing up after a meal can quickly dispose of leftover food on plates before stacking them in the dishwasher. This arrangement will cause minimum disruption.

Family kitchens are subject to wear and tear, especially where space is restricted. Choose good materials and sturdy cabinets that are designed to last.

Single galleys only have sufficient space for one family member to work in the kitchen at a time. A microwave and refrigerator placed toward the end of the run allow children to fetch drinks and heat snacks without obstructing the main work flow.

Utilize the limited space by installing floor to ceiling cabinets and by choosing compact appliances. Extend the food preparation area with a large chopping block that fits neatly over the sink top.

If the two-wall galley kitchen can be accessed from both ends, consider blocking up one door to prevent children from using the kitchen as a corridor and racing through the room from one end to the other, which may cause accidents.

Two-wall galleys do not have the space for a family table so other eating arrangements will have to be made. Bear in mind that by placing cutlery, dishes, and glasses in base cabinets they are more accessible to children.

Kitchens can be hazardous places for children, so pay attention to safety when the kitchen is being built and also when it is up and running.

When undertaking structural work, consider making a pass-through from the kitchen into the adjacent living/dining area. This is useful for transferring drinks and food from one room to the other, and is also an ideal way to keep a watchful eye on young children while you are busy preparing food.

As there is little space in a galley kitchen, place the refrigerator and microwave in an adjacent room throughout the building work for preparing family meals.

To help keep surfaces clear in the limited space of a two-wall galley, install a faucet with a built-in filtering system when you plan your kitchen plumbing. In cooking, the filtered water improves the flavor of food.

Although natural stone flooring is expensive, the small floor area of a two-walled galley makes it affordable. The floor needs at least 24 hours to settle and set so make sure that all the family meals are organized for eating out or home delivery.

KEY

🔲 planning   🔶 utilities   🗄 storage   ⊞ appliances   ◔ small appliances

🔳 furniture   ⬛ surfaces   ✦ flooring   ⊞ windows   🔦 lighting

L-SHAPE

🔲 This kitchen shape is practical for families as it divides easily into kitchen and eating area. Food preparation can take place on one side of the room, while younger family members can sit at a table on the other side where they can be supervised.

🔲 In L-shaped kitchens, several family members can work together at the same time if the food rinsing and preparation area is located in a separate cabinet run to the stove, and there is plenty of free counter space.

🔲 If the L-shaped kitchen sits in a large room, consider planning a separate island for food preparation and casual meals. With this arrangement, older children can prepare and eat snacks at the island and clean up afterward with little fuss.

🗄 Children's games and toys scattered over the large floor area of an L-shaped room can cause accidents. Plan a pull-out chest in the kitchen for toy storage so that they can be put away neatly at mealtimes.

⬛ If you have an L-shaped kitchen that projects into a larger room, choose kitchen countertops with rounded edges so that young children will not knock themselves against any sharp corners.

🔳 If your L-shaped kitchen is part of a large family room, buy dust covers or use old sheets to protect new sofas, armchairs, and other soft furnishings from dust and paint splashes when the final decorating and fitting jobs are being done.

U-SHAPE

🔲 If the corners of the U-shape seem gloomy even in daylight, choose pale-colored cabinet finishes to help reflect light around the kitchen room. For family kitchens, make sure that the cabinets have a hard wearing finish that will withstand regular cleaning of scuffs and fingermarks.

🗄 In U-shaped rooms there is often space for a tall cabinet. Store a platform step inside for children so that they can reach the sink to wash their hands before meals.

🗄 Plan pull-out storage cabinets for non-perishable food items so that young children can easily see and reach items inside. Place the frequently used food storage cabinets away from the deep corners of a U-shaped kitchen so that access is not restricted.

🔲 Where U-shaped kitchens extend to form a peninsula, utilize the extra counter space to create a breakfast bar with stools where casual meals can be enjoyed out of the cook's work path.

🔲 Refitting a large U-shaped family kitchen involves a lot of disruption. Pack away kitchen equipment to keep it dust-free, and try to keep the refrigerator and microwave up and running.

✦ U-shaped kitchens often have a smaller floor area than L-shaped and island kitchens which makes expensive flooring materials like natural stone more affordable. When mortar is used, the kitchen will be off limits to adults and children for 24–48 hours while it sets.

ISLAND

🔲 Family members should be able to move freely around the island without obstruction. To prevent injury, choose rounded edges for your island counter, particularly if it is at the same level as the head-height of children.

🔲 If the stove is contained within the island, fit a high protective backsplash around the stovetop cooking area so that young children snacking at the island when you are cooking are adequately protected from hot splashes of water or fat.

🔲 If you choose to serve your children meals at the island, make sure that your choice of chairs or stools are the correct height and have a back rest and side bars so that they can sit comfortably and safely at the counter.

⊞ Large families may require the capacity of a commercial double refrigerator. Make sure that there is plenty of room between the island and refrigerator so that the large double doors can open fully without knocking into the surrounding cabinetry.

✦ Remember that fitting discreet downdraft ventilation into the island cooktop rather than placing a large ventilation hood above the island may cause major disruption in a family kitchen as the flooring has to be taken up to lay the ducting pipes.

🔶 If the island contains both a single sink and a cooktop, bear in mind that gas and water supplies will have to be fed under the floor before the island is installed, and this can be quite expensive.

Assessing your space: special needs

Safety and accessibility are key factors to consider when choosing and planning a kitchen for those with special needs.

 SMALL KITCHEN

 LARGE KITCHEN

Consider the specific needs of the person who will use the kitchen, bearing in mind any sight or other physical challenges they may have to overcome.

- In a narrow galley kitchen, check that there will be sufficient space for a wheelchair to pass through even when base cabinet and appliance doors are open.

- If the user is visually impaired, consider whether contrasting surfaces on cabinets and knobs will help define areas.

- Consider kitchen appliances – especially stoves and ranges with clearly marked, easily operated control panels.

- For a physically challenged adult, a large kitchen can be difficult to move around in. Arrange the major appliances in a practical, short work triangle. The leftover space will provide useful storage for items not frequently used.

- A large room will have space for a table. Choose a table at a suitable height for wheelchair access. A pedestal table, which has one central leg, is less obstructive.

A kitchen designed for those with special needs does not have to look utilitarian. Many good-looking products are designed to make life easier for everyone.

- If the kitchen is for the use of other family members too, make sure that that there is a choice of counter heights.

- Good lighting will help to highlight activity areas and draw attention to dangers such as spills and splashes. Avoid reflective surfaces that make seeing items more difficult.

- Make sure that the controls are easy to turn. A pull-out hand spray is useful as is a faucet close to the range to fill pans for cooking.

- To save energy when working in a large kitchen, choose faucets controlled by an electronic sensor or those with wrist levers.

- Consider whether a drop-down or side-opening oven door will aid or restrict access. Drop-down doors provide a useful ledge when taking hot food out of the oven.

- For large areas, choose a non-slip cushioned vinyl flooring material or linoleum which is soft, quiet, and inexpensive to buy.

It is important to make sure that someone who has special needs can still have access to cooking facilities while the new kitchen is being installed.

- Consider fitting a hot-water dispenser when the sink and plumbing are installed so that the kettle does not have to be lifted, filled, and boiled each time a hot drink or hot water is required.

- When installing small kitchens, fit grip bars next to the sink area and cooktop where the user may be required to stand for periods of time. If adapting an existing kitchen, fit grip bars where the extra security of a handhold is required and there is space.

- When lighting is being installed, make sure that switches are visible and easy to reach from a wheelchair. Two-way electrical switches operated from both sides of the kitchen will minimize travel across the room.

- To reduce the amount of cleaning in a large kitchen for those with special needs, reserve tiles for low-wear backsplash areas. Grout between floor and counter tiles in large areas can harbor crumbs and residues making them hard to clean.

KITCHEN STYLES

Choosing a style

When you have assessed your lifestyle and planned how best to use the available space, it is time to consider the visual and practical aspects of selecting kitchen furniture. Your choice of cabinets and materials should reflect your needs.

cross refer to
design your kitchen 34
kitchen materials 84
wall surfaces 86
cabinet finishes 94

Start formulating your ideas and style preferences by looking through magazines and manufacturers' brochures, or browsing the internet. Compile a portfolio of pictures of products that would suit you. Before making any decisions, ask to see samples and visit kitchen showrooms.

Modern versus traditional

Convenience and efficiency are key elements in a modern kitchen. A battery of hi-tech appliances and gadgetry tucked behind sleek cabinets are perfect for those who like a clean, no-fuss approach to kitchens. For many, the charm of a traditionally styled kitchen is more appealing. Many modern appliances are designed to blend unobtrusively into a traditional kitchen, or are easily disguised by clever cabinetry.

Built-in or freestanding?

A well-planned, built-in kitchen, with standard or custom-made cabinets, will utilize every inch of space, making it ideal for small or irregular-shaped rooms. A freestanding kitchen is less formal and offers the opportunity to use various pieces of furniture to add interest. However, separate items take up more space.

Materials and finishes

Whatever materials and finishes you choose for your kitchen, check that they are designed to withstand the wear and tear they will receive. While hi-gloss lacquer and wood veneers are suitable for kitchens receiving light use, those in constant use will need heavier duty, more hard-wearing products made from stainless steel and solid wood.

Kitchen hardware

The smallest detail can make a huge difference to the overall look of your kitchen. Cabinet hardware should enhance the color and texture of the finish as well as being comfortable to use. Traditional china knobs, hand-carved handles, or contemporary metalwork designs can contribute a sophisticated or quirky touch to the most inexpensive cabinet.

1 This freestanding bench combines several materials to make it both practical and hard wearing. It is strong and lightweight, allowing it to be lifted forward for regular cleaning.

3 Staggered cabinet levels combined with opaque and colored cabinet doors add visual interest to this simple contemporary kitchen. The choice of gleaming hardware is a small detail but provides the essential finishing touch.

2 Combining traditional style with a built-in layout has turned this room into a practical family kitchen. Activity centers on the range which contrasts with the cabinets to create a strong focal point.

KITCHEN PLANNING

Design your kitchen

You will need to work out a successful plan that includes your chosen kitchen furniture and appliances. Take ideas from the kitchens featured in this book, then use the graph paper and stickers and try out various layouts to find the best one for you.

The principles behind good kitchen design are intended to maximize efficiency, function, convenience, and safety. It may seem an impossible task to achieve this goal, especially when there are constraints on space and budget. Whatever the limitations, the time spent at the planning stage will reduce the chances of making costly mistakes that will only need to be fixed at a later date. When you feel confident about your ideas, put them into practice by drawing up the plans. Use the following guidelines to make sure that the kitchen you design is highly efficient, easy, and convenient to use on a daily basis.

Drawing up a plan

It is essential to draw accurate floor plans of the existing room before planning any new kitchen. You will need to take several measurements of the room and transfer them onto the graph paper to make an exact scale plan.

Standing in the center of the room, start by drawing a rough sketch of the floor area, including architectural features or items of furniture that are to remain. Measure the floor area, and note the width and length clearly on the sketch. Next, measure each wall length in turn, working in a clockwise direction, adding the dimensions to the relevant parts of your sketch.

Mark on your plans exactly where the utility points – gas, electrical outlets, and water supply – are situated on each wall. You may find a symbol such as a flame for gas, a zigzag for electricity, and a teardrop shape for water useful if one area on the plan is cramped.

Wall elevations

You will also need to note wall elevations. Measure the height and width of each wall, then draw a rough sketch, adding details including the windows, doors, built-in bookcases, ventilation outlets, and radiators. Mark each sketch with a letter A, B, and so on. Draw up the elevation to scale on graph paper. Put the corresponding letter against the wall it relates to on the floor plan for reference.

Structural changes

You may feel that the space in your kitchen is limited and restricts your design. Look at the possibilities of making two rooms into one large one or pushing out a wall to create a light, airy garden room. It will allow greater choice when planning the new kitchen layout, and could

4 All the activity zones in this one-wall galley kitchen receive good natural daylight from the window and glass door. Placing the hood against an outside wall maximizes its efficiency and also limits ducting.

provide space for an eating area. Large rooms are ideal for including a "soft" seating area where everyone can congregate and be safely away from cooking activities.

Most remodeling is done within the confines of a budget. But there is no substitute for quality, so consult your architect or remodeling contractor, who will advise on the best way of going about structural changes. It is better to get the basics of building, utilities, and cabinetry absolutely right from the start – you can always upgrade seating and accessories at a later date. Meet budgets by bearing the hidden costs in mind. For example, placing appliances requiring plumbing along one wall will reduce installation costs. Ducting from a hood is also cheaper to install if situated against an outside wall rather than ducted from an island across the room.

DESIGN POINTS

◪ Start by placing the sink cabinet on your kitchen plan (it is usually the longest cabinet) and arrange the dishwasher close by.

◪ Arrange the food preparation area and cooking area near the sink to form an efficient work triangle. The sink should be placed so that pans do not have to be carried far.

◪ Plan the food preparation area between the sink and cooktop, allowing space for rinsed items to be transferred easily from the sink to the counter and onto the cooktop.

◪ Position the refrigerator within easy reach of the kitchen table or food preparation zone.

◪ If there is space for a separate table, try to locate it near a window so it's exposed to natural daylight.

Kitchen shapes

Whatever the shape of kitchen, it will be more efficient if planned with an understanding of the work triangle. On your plan, mark a point in the center of each activity zone, such as the refrigerator, cooktop, and sink, and draw a line to link them. The triangle may be asymmetrical but ideally, each line should be between 4ft and 9ft (1.2 and 2.7m) long when scaled up to your kitchen's proportions.

cross refer to
wall cabinets 36
base cabinets 38
cooktops & hoods 74
countertops 92

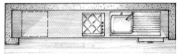

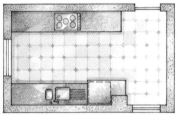

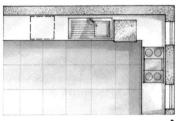

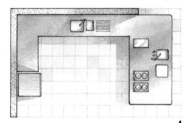

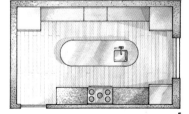

1 Plan the layout of a galley kitchen so there is a preparation area between the cooktop and refrigerator. Leave enough space in the corner to allow elbow room and space for long pan handles.

2 A refrigerator at the end of a run of cabinets, away from the main activity area, allows the appliance to be used without restricting the movement of the cook.

3 Keep plumbing runs and ventilation ducting short to reduce costs and maximize efficiency. Here, the dishwasher is plumbed in next to the sink and the hood is against an external wall.

4 Space for a wide counter area offers extra depth for a separate cooktop and a second small rinsing sink to be positioned opposite one another.

5 Two work triangles function easily within this kitchen's central island design. The first links the cooktop, refrigerator, and central sink; on the opposite wall, food and equipment can be taken from the cabinets to the island for preparation.

Wall cabinets

Efficiently planned wall cabinets should be easy to reach and offer flexible storage. They are most useful for light kitchen equipment and tableware but provide an ideal spot to keep seasonings, oils, and other staples above the food preparation area.

Wall cabinets provide an essential storage area for different types of kitchen equipment and the non-perishable food you keep in stock. The internal fittings need to be arranged differently from those in base cabinets to prevent shelves from being overstacked, which could result in items tumbling out as the door is opened. They are less practical the farther they extend beyond head height, since goods cannot be reached easily.

Narrow solutions

Wall cabinets are usually half the depth of base cabinets to allow the countertop below to be used comfortably without restricting headroom. The top of wall cabinets can often end up becoming just a surface for collecting dust. To keep surfaces clear, and clutter out of sight, consider installing full-height wall cabinets that fit flush to the ceiling. If you do decide on this option, it would be practical to include storage for a stepladder in your plans so that the highest shelves can be reached safely and easily.

Unless the kitchen has more than one source of natural daylight, do not be tempted to fit wall cabinets right up to edge of the window recess. Solid cabinets close to windows will prevent the light from entering the kitchen, casting much of the room in deep shadow. Where lack of space dictates that cabinets have to be close to windows, choose a style of cabinet where the sides and doors have opaque glass to allow the light to filter through.

2

4

3

5

1 To relieve the monotony of repetitive cabinetry, a combination of solid and glass-door fronts and staggered cabinet heights have been used to create a country-style kitchen.

2 Discreet halogen downlights fitted into the base of the wall cabinets provide accent lighting for a collection of china displayed on the shelving below.

3 A freestanding tall pantry cabinet makes full use of the available wall space. The cabinet doors are fitted with opaque glass to allow a glimpse of the items stored inside.

4 Custom-made shelves are complemented by the smaller cabinet on the adjacent wall. This open cabinet allows everything to be seen at a glance but requires regular cleaning to remove dust and grease to keep its appearance.

5 Fluorescent strip lighting casts clear, shadowless light onto the food preparation area beneath. To prevent eyestrain, the strips should not be visible when standing at the counter.

6 To prevent plates from being stacked too high inside cabinets, provide a series of shelves. Vary the space between the shelves to allow tall and low items to be stored and reached with ease.

7 The best position for storage cabinets is between knee and eye level. Consider roll-out pantry cabinets if you use a lot of small items such as cans and bottles for everyday cooking.

DESIGN POINTS

Undercabinet lights are ideal for illuminating countertops. Whether you choose fluorescent strips or low-voltage halogen lights, make sure that they are shielded to prevent glare.

The distance between the countertop and bottom of the wall cabinets should be decided by your height and reach. Ideally, items stored on the top shelf of a cabinet should be visible, but cabinets situated too low on the wall will restrict headroom and countertop access.

Wallmounted plate racks are useful for storage, and the plates are less likely to chip than those stacked in piles. The disadvantage of open plate racks is that unless the plates are used regularly, they will soon collect dust.

cross refer to
food storage areas 56
storing kitchenware 58
storing utility items 68
changing cabinets 100

8 This dresser combines traditional features including cup hooks and plate racks to offer a versatile range of practical and attractive storage options.

9 Utilize the wallspace between the countertop and wall cabinets by fitting a utensil rack, narrow drawers, or shelving. Special steel-grid systems are available that fit flush to the wall and provide space for utensils to be hung up ready for use.

10 Where fragile items are displayed on open shelving, choose a railed front to prevent them from falling off. The classic carved detail, shown here, makes an attractive frame for the interesting collection of preserves.

Base cabinets

Base cabinets must be tough and durable, since they receive the real wear and tear in kitchens. Doors must withstand constant opening and closing, and the internal fittings should be able to take the heaviest pans and dishes.

From the surface of the countertop to the toe space at floor level, base cabinets are regularly subjected to knocks, splashes, and kitchen chemicals. But it is the frame that takes the weight of the countertop, doors, and equipment, so choose the best you can afford. There is a choice of cabinets. Stock cabinets are factory-produced and come in a range of standard sizes that can be put together in any combination. Custom-built cabinets will be tailored to exactly the dimensions of a wall or recess, which is particularly useful for uneven walls and floors.

Material matters

The frame is simply a box with height-adjustable feet or wall-mounting brackets and shelves. Plywood, particleboard, medium-density fiberboard (MDF), or a combination, is widely used in the construction. They are not necessarily cheaper than solid wood, but will not twist, shrink, or split with changes in heat and humidity and are easy to wipe clean. Hardwoods are often chosen for the framework and joints to add strength and rigidity.

Cabinets with one top drawer and door are more expensive than full-height doors because of the work and fittings involved in production. Drawer cabinets are good for storing small equipment, utensils, and supplies. Storage racks, carousels, and slide-out, open-weave fruit and vegetable baskets are just some of the useful internal fittings available that keep items tidy and allow the contents to be seen clearly at a glance.

1 An arrangement of graduated drawers and cupboards have been chosen to reflect the needs of the cook. Small individual spice drawers situated immediately beneath the counter have a simple, functional finger-hole pull.

2 A pull-out chiller cabinet situated close to the food preparation area keeps fruit and salads fresh and crisp.

3 This series of small drawers is ideal for keeping seasonings and small utensils close to the cooking area.

4 The simple lines of this modern base cabinet are echoed by the choice of kitchenware.

5 Mock drawer fronts harmonize with the surrounding fitted cabinets but conceal an innovative set of pull-out drawers to provide full access to the contents at every level.

6 Here, plain modern wooden doors have simple stainless steel handles. There is no visible face frame and all the hinges are concealed.

7 Plan to have a range of drawer dividers to help to separate small and large utensils.

8 A bread drawer has a lid that doubles as a board, and a removable liner to empty crumbs.

DESIGN POINTS

The kickspace enables the user to stand in front of the base cabinet. A plinth hides the adjustable legs and seals the gap between the floor and cabinet. Modern cabinets have legs that are designed to be seen, creating a lighter, spacious look. Dust can collect underneath, so the floor will require regular cleaning.

If the kitchen is small or irregularly shaped, look for special narrow-width cabinets that will utilize every available inch of space.

For a fully integrated kitchen you may want to consider panels that fit on the front of appliances. Some are designed to fit into a frame on the appliance door, or the appliance can be concealed behind a cabinet door. Panels are not recommended for use with hot appliances.

Wine racks are only really useful for wines that need to be served at room temperature. The temperature changes in most kitchens can speed the deterioration of good wines.

Frameless or Eurostyle cabinets have no visible face frame, and all the hinges are concealed. They are as durable as traditional-framed cabinets but create a plainer look and also uninterrupted access to the interior.

5

8

9

10

6

7

cross refer to
choosing a style 16
food storage areas 56
storing kitchenware 58
changing cabinets 100

9 A wine rack can be installed below the countertop to make use of an awkward or narrow space.

10 Include a set of shallow drawers in your plan if you need to store a collection of kitchen utensils and linens.

11 A narrow pull-out cabinet is useful for storing tall bottles containing vinegars and oils, and containers of herbs or spices.

11

Great kitchen rooms

Planning the layout for a spacious kitchen room can be as much of an ergonomic challenge as planning a compact kitchen. Aim to incorporate separate areas for work and relaxation so others can share the kitchen and remain out of harm's way.

Approach the design of a large kitchen as with any other: selecting specific areas for food preparation, cooking, eating, and relaxing zones. Use a dining table, an island, or sofa to create a natural divide between the kitchen and the living area so that each part can function separately.

A large kitchen needs a strong focal point around which the various activities revolve. Avoid placing all kitchen cabinets and activity zones around the perimeter walls as this will create a lot of "dead space" in the middle of a large room. Instead, concentrate the activities in one area so that the user does not have to waste time and energy walking large distances from one activity zone to the next. Where there is sufficient space, a central island for food preparation, cooking, and eating is ergonomic as it concentrates activity in the center of the room.

Appliances

Large-scale, commercial appliances have the right proportions to look comfortable in a good-size room, so take advantage of the wide range on offer. In large kitchens, consider installing features such as a second, smaller sink to take the pressure off the main sink. This back-up sink can be used by others for rinsing salads or glasses before refilling them.

When deciding whether to site the cooktop or range in an island or on an outside wall, bear in mind how the extractor hood and overhead ducting may affect the impressive proportions of a large kitchen.

Remember to plan the position of the refrigerator away from heat sources and close to the eating and relaxing area as it will be used by everyone, and it is important to keep general traffic away from food preparation and cooking areas.

Light sources

To avoid shadowy areas in the center of a big room and in activity areas, natural and artificial lighting has to be well planned. Generally, it is best to place the eating area where windows or glass doors offer natural daylight. However, you may prefer this location for your sink or food preparation areas. Positioned away from natural light sources, the eating area will benefit from a lighting installation that offers clear and subdued light levels for all occasions.

Linking areas

A grand kitchen room should look attractive as well as being functional. Clever use of color and materials will link work and relaxation areas, and by using similar materials throughout you will make sure that the room's style is consistent.

1 A bar sink between the double-fronted unit enables glasses to be rinsed and drinks to be made close to the table without encroaching on the main kitchen area.

2 The position of the table benefits from natural light and, with the banquette beneath the window, offers seats at the table or just a casual place to relax.

1

cross refer to
choosing a style 16
design your kitchen 34
activity areas 54
serving & eating 66

4 The kitchen area is situated at the far end of this room with the cooking zone placed against an outside wall to benefit from minimal ducting. The table is placed in the window allowing for maximum daylight exposure.

3

3 Divided into distinct areas, this layout is ideal for large, sociable kitchens; allowing the cook to face and talk to others in the seating and eating areas.

DESIGN POINTS

To add interest to solid color door and drawer fronts, combine open shelf and glass-fronted cabinets to break the monotony of repetitive cabinetry.

Install a colored flooring, counters or backsplash that enhances not merges with the cabinets.

Aim to have a point of interest within the room; a colorful refrigerator, antique table or collection of kitchenware could be all that is needed to create a comfortable, well-furnished room.

Because of the different thicknesses of hard and soft flooring materials available, it is practical to use the same flooring throughout the kitchen and living areas. A rug or carpet in the dining or relaxing area will add comfort and create a relaxed, informal look.

4

One-wall galley

With clever planning and resourcefulness, a single line of cabinets can function as an efficient, streamlined kitchen. The location of the sink, cooktop, and refrigerator is the key to a successful layout, and the detail you choose will create the kitchen's style.

1 Galley kitchens require imaginative use of wall and floor space to function efficiently. Here, pans, utensils, plates, and glasses are stacked on an open rack above the counter which is narrow enough not to restrict headroom.

In a single-line or one-wall galley kitchen, the work triangle concept does not apply. Movement is linear from one activity area to the next. For ease of use, it is advisable to separate the cooking and washing zones by a length of worksurface. However, resist the temptation to place the sink or oven at opposite ends of the run in order to gain a larger counter area, or you will feel restricted and your movements will be compromised. There must be sufficient room to set down hot pans on either side of the stove area, and space for pan handles to slightly project over the edge of the cooktop without becoming a hazard. To maintain an uninterrupted work space, plan below-counter appliances such as a compact refrigerator, oven, and dishwasher, and use any remaining space to fit base cabinets for storing heavy pans and electric appliances.

Space considerations

Where two people intend to cook side by side, a one-wall galley of cabinets and appliances may restrict movement. Prevent the limited space from becoming a nuisance by planning a pull-out cart (see p.52) that can be used as a separate food preparation area by one of the cooks. If you also need an informal eating area in the kitchen, a fold-out breakfast bar and stacking stools are useful as they can be stowed away after the meal is over.

If possible, try to plan an extra-deep countertop along the length of the galley kitchen so that you can store equipment along the back edge without interrupting the work area. Consider an appliance garage with built-in electric outlets and a roll-top door. Use it to store the food processor, blender, toaster, and other appliances when not in use.

2 A galley kitchen fitted under the roof eaves of this attic utilizes the limited space to create a functional work area with adequate headroom.

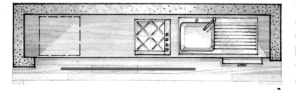

DESIGN POINTS

Where space is restricted, do not be tempted to place the cooktop or sink in the corner as there will be insufficient room for you to use either comfortably or safely.

Utilize the mid-height wall space between the countertop and wall cabinets by fitting a single rail for hanging kitchen utensils.

If the kitchen is part of a larger living area, it can be screened off with shutters or a remote-controlled aluminum venetian shade that will reflect light and make the kitchen appear more spacious.

A tall, floor-to-ceiling pull-out pantry will hold a surprising amount of food. Hidden behind cabinetry, it will appear less obtrusive in a small space. Position it at the end of a run of base cabinets so that when the pantry doors are open it will not obstruct or restrict movement around the rest of the kitchen.

4 The curved shape of this kitchen counteracts the uniformity of a conventional straight run of cabinets, creating visual interest. The curved design also has ergonomic advantages in that the cook does not have to walk so far between activity areas.

5 A wall of fitted cabinets and appliances mixes dark and light finishes with stainless steel to create a dramatic effect. The curved cooktop and hood are lit by halogen downlights recessed in the plinth above, making a striking focal point.

6 A flip-down table and stacking chairs turn this long, narrow galley kitchen into a cozy dining area for two at mealtimes.

3 Plan the work line of a one-wall galley kitchen to include an area with a minimum run of 18in (45cm) between the sink and cooktop. Position the refrigerator underneath the food preparation area for easy access, and the dishwasher close to the sink to keep plumbing costs down.

Two-wall galley

The ergonomic success of galley kitchens lies in the simple but efficient use of space that they provide. Plan storage and appliances within specific activity areas to make sure that it is easy to move from one side of the room to the other.

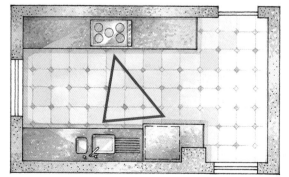

Sometimes referred to as a "corridor kitchen," a two wall galley consists of two facing walls with cabinetry and/or appliances along both. Consider the effectiveness of a ship's galley and it is evident that the principles governing the basic layout work well, even in the most confined space.

The one time when a kitchen layout such as this is not so practical is when doors are situated at both ends of the room. This creates a busy corridor that others must use to reach internal rooms or to go outdoors. It is tolerable for a couple but impractical for families, since the constant movement can disrupt the smooth flow of those working in the kitchen and create potential hazards.

Efficient workspace

An efficient work triangle is fairly easy to achieve between two walls, but plan it taking your needs into account. Assess how often you use each of the appliances. If you cook often and prepare everything from fresh ingredients, it is best to keep the main countertop area between the oven and sink clear for food preparation. Position a side-by-side refrigerator and deep-freezer under the counter, where they are easily reached, or if you prefer a tall fridge-freezer, place it against the facing wall to keep the work area free. Avoid placing refrigerators and deep freezers next to cooktops or ranges as the different temperatures will conflict, making them less efficient. If you have no other option, make sure that there is sufficient insulation between the two appliances.

The distance between facing cabinets should be no less than 42in (105cm), the minimum needed to use appliances with room for others to pass safely. Items requiring plumbing, such as the dishwasher and sink, should be close together to limit the length of plumbing runs. The same applies for ventilation ducting, so plan the position of the cooktop, oven, or range against an exterior wall to keep ducting minimal.

1 Place the refrigerator close to the door so that groceries can be quickly unloaded and others can use it without disrupting the smooth work flow.

2 Contrasting colors add interest to the simple, practical layout of this two-wall galley kitchen. The Shaker peg-rail provides an attractive storage solution, and echoes the wall cabinets' finish. Space at the end of the kitchen is used for a cane armchair and a narrow display shelf for decorative kitchenware.

3 A typical two-wall galley kitchen layout shows the relationship between the main activity areas to create an efficient work triangle. The position of the cooking area, sink, and refrigerator are served by separate stretches of countertop.

cross refer to
design your kitchen 34
one-wall galley 42
selecting equipment 70
lighting 88

4 Plenty of space and natural daylight offset the deep-plum-colored cabinets and woodwork. The angle and depth of the base cabinets and the wide countertop are ideal for food preparation and storing small appliances.

5 Making use of a larger room, this galley kitchen enables the cook to talk to guests seated opposite. Two-way cabinets facing into the living area contain plates and glassware that can be removed without crossing the kitchen work path.

6 A choice of cabinets with staggered depth and height achieves a perfect solution for a variety of cooking activities and storage requirements. Skylights allow light to filter down into the room for clear, shadowless countertops.

DESIGN POINTS

Where space between the two facing walls is greater than 48in (122cm), it is possible to use a wider counter that will double up as a breakfast bar for family meals.

A full-height pantry is best placed at the end of the run of cabinets, next to the wall. The solid block of cabinetry involved in their construction can make a small galley look cramped and obstruct a smooth work flow.

Add an element of interest to break up the uniform shape of two-wall galley kitchens by installing angled or curved base and wall cabinets at the ends of a run. This will also create more space at the point at which you enter a narrow two-wall galley kitchen and help the flow of movement into and out of the kitchen area.

It may not be feasible to include a permanent eating area in a two-wall galley kitchen as space may be limited, so choose a folding table and chairs that can be put away when not in use.

L-shaped kitchens

Kitchens based on an L-shaped layout form a natural work triangle between the adjacent walls. The layout is easily adapted to suit both compact spaces or larger rooms, where a seating or dining area can be accommodated easily in the free space.

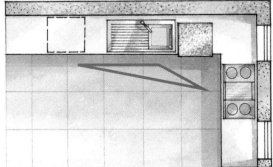

1 A neat work triangle is created between the tall fridge-freezer, freestanding table, and built-in cooking zone. Good insulation between the fridge-freezer and oven creates a heatproof barrier that allows for their close proximity.

An L-shaped layout allows space for a table and seating without blocking the work path between the main activity zones. With careful planning, a folding table and chairs can be fitted into a small room for casual meals, or to provide an extra worksurface when needed.

Consider first where the doors and windows are situated since they will have a bearing on the best position for activity areas. For safety, the cooking zone, including the range or built-in oven, cooktop, and microwave, should not be placed immediately next to a doorway. If possible, plan the refrigerator's or fridge-freezer's position toward the end of a run of cabinets near to the door so that groceries can be brought in and unpacked easily. This also allows others general access to cold drinks and snacks without interrupting the natural work path.

New angles

The internal angle of an L-shaped kitchen requires careful consideration for practical storage solutions. It is an area that is difficult to reach and usually too deep to see into clearly. Drawers opening across the right angle can only be used one at a time and an open dishwasher door will obstruct access to adjacent cabinets. To overcome and accommodate these limitations, several swing-out tray designs and revolving shelves are available, which make locating kitchen equipment easier. Other alternatives such as a diagonally positioned sink, cooktop, or range with a counter on either side and

storage beneath also make good use of the space and create a strong focal point.

Allow as much natural light into the room as possible. This can be a problem if wall space next to the windows is required for cabinets; in this case, choose open or glass-fronted cabinets or plate racks to utilize the space. Alternatively, fit a system of hooks or shelves which will not reduce light levels to the wall.

2 Placing the cooktop, oven, and hood on the outside wall is key to this layout. Light from the windows illuminates the main activity zones throughout the day.

3 The washing, cooking, and refrigeration areas form the corners of this work triangle.

cross refer to

wall cabinets 36
activity areas 54
serving & eating 66
lighting 88

DESIGN POINTS

❖ Flooring in the kitchen must be durable, but adding a non-slip rug or mat will make the dining area cozier.

◪ Make sure that the lighting you choose can be altered from what is needed in a kitchen's busy working environment to what is desirable to create a relaxed atmosphere for dining. The simplest arrangement can be operated by a dimmer switch, or you can install two separate systems to provide task lighting and soft, mood lighting that focuses on the table.

▥ If there is space for a freestanding table, look for a pedestal design or one where the legs are fixed away from the edges so that they are less likely to be bumped into, and the chairs when not needed can be tucked well underneath.

◩ Where the counter projects beyond an activity zone, consider using the surface for a combination countertop/ breakfast bar with stacking stools.

4 Placing the large porcelain sink in the center of the countertop allows space for rinsing and preparing vegetables and for stacking large pots for washing.

5 The smooth lines and hardwearing materials used in this kitchen make it ideal for busy cooks. A table and chairs provide comfortable seating for preparation jobs and for meals.

4

5

U-shaped kitchens

By arranging your kitchen elements in a U-shape, cabinets and appliances are set around three sides of the room with access from one side only. This layout works well for both large and small kitchen areas providing the corner spaces are well utilized.

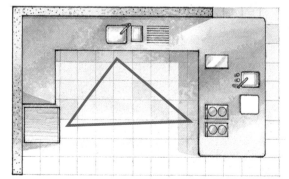

1

Planning an efficient workspace within a U-shaped kitchen is easy in an average-sized room providing that the kitchen activity zones are only a few paces from one another. For maximum efficiency in large U-shaped rooms, aim to locate the key appliances: oven, sink, and refrigerator within a work triangle, where each item sits no more than 9ft (3m) away from one another. This will help reduce the amount of time and energy spent traveling across the room when working in the kitchen for long periods of time.

When planning the layout, position the dishwasher, cooktop, and built-in oven toward the center of the countertops. These appliances should stand well away from the entrance and corners of the room so that access to them is unrestricted. Check that when the appliances are open, they do not obstruct adjacent base or wall cabinets. And, if possible, place the refrigerator at the end of a run of cabinets so that other people can take chilled drinks and snacks from the refrigerator without obstructing the work path. A specially designed double-sink unit that fits neatly into a corner space (see p.79) may offer an ergonomic solution to planning a small but functional U-shaped kitchen.

Table arrangements

Large U-shaped rooms have enough floor space to accommodate a central table for eating, while still allowing room for the cook to work. For small U-shaped kitchens, where there is insufficient space for a permanent

eating area, a foldaway table is more practical. Plan a pull-out table that can be stored in the space between the countertop and base cabinet, and keep folding chairs in a tall storage cabinet. Aim to locate the eating area close to a window so that it receives natural daylight. Dark corners can be a problem in U-shaped kitchens. Avoid working in shadow by planning directional task lights in these areas to diffuse lighting over surfaces.

2

1 A U-shaped kitchen in a large room offers an efficient, contained workspace. Cabinets facing the dining area store tableware where it can be easily reached. A low-level cooktop makes it easy for the cook to check the contents of pans while talking to family or friends seated around the table.

2 By placing a double-width countertop along one side of the kitchen, a second sink for rinsing fresh ingredients, and a gas ring cooktop and pan rest can be incorporated into the kitchen design. These facilities can be reached from both sides of the workbench. Space below the countertop provides ample storage for less frequently used food preparation equipment.

3 A diagram of the U-shaped kitchen (in picture 2) shows the flow of movement between the built-in refrigerator, cooktop, and the sink zone. Refrigerated ingredients need only be transported a short distance for rinsing and cooking.

3

cross refer to
wall cabinets 36
serving & eating 66
sinks & faucets 78
lighting 88

4

5

DESIGN POINTS

If the kitchen is small, plan a bi-fold door or one that slides into a pocket or space recessed in the wall. A door that opens into the kitchen will only restrict access to appliances or obstruct the nearest countertop.

Where space is at a premium, select compact kitchen appliances such as dishwashers and refrigerators that are narrower than standard.

Install a single sink recessed into the countertop without a draining board, to make sure that there is still a large counter area free for food preparation. Make sure that the counter adjoining the sink without a draining board is water-resistant.

If possible, plan a lower section of countertop so that you can bear down on jobs that require some effort, such as rolling pastry, chopping vegetables, and kneading bread.

4 Tapering the end cabinets improves access and the flow of traffic in a narrow U-shaped kitchen. Here, open racks are used for wine storage so bottles can be kept at room temperature.

5 Narrow shelves above the sink cabinet do not restrict the users' headroom or block the natural light from the window in this compact but functional kitchen.

6 A freestanding larder cupboard lends a "furnished" look to this bespoke kitchen. The U-shape maintains an efficient work area but opens out into a living-room so that the cook can interact with guests.

6

Island kitchens

Island kitchen designs are efficient work stations for cooks, since they combine several activities within a small area. They are ideal as part of a larger room where the family can congregate and join in with the preparation of meals.

1

The simplest island could be a wooden butcher's block providing an additional preparation surface, or a sophisticated unit comprising appliances, equipment, storage, and a ventilation system. Whatever you choose, it must be possible to move around it freely, without interrupting the smooth work path between adjacent activity zones.

One of the benefits of an island layout is that it provides more space for two people to move easily around the kitchen, since all sides of the island can be utilized. It also allows the cook to face into the room and participate in conversation rather than be isolated from the group, and often doubles as a place for friends to sit and help prepare meals.

A central island should have at least 3ft 10in (118cm) between it and facing wall cabinets so that it is possible for two to work in comfort. Make sure that the natural path from the door of the room does not entail circumnavigating the island, since this will make it awkward to move easily in and out of the living area.

Working space

The number of appliances and amount of storage you include in the design of the island is a matter of personal choice, but allow space between the key activities for pans to be set down and ingredients to be kept close by. It is useful to vary the height of the counter by including one or two low-level areas. The main reason for this is that some kitchen activities are much more comfortable and easier to undertake at a lower level: it is also a suitable area for children to do their schoolwork or join in other kitchen activities.

Consider the type of materials best suited to your style of cooking to make food preparation efficient. A marble or granite area stays cool, and can be wiped clean, making it ideal for preparing fish and pastry. A stainless-steel or terrazzo insert is tough and heat resistant, so hot pans can be left on top without damage.

1 Storage space is maximized within this island so that all the equipment needed for food preparation is easily accessible. The suspended hanging rack has been designed with smaller dimensions, so as not to obstruct the cook, and holds a collection of decorative kitchenware to make an eye-catching display.

2 A minimalist-style, brushed stainless-steel island provides a simple, effective, and highly durable work area. The sink is set at one end, freeing the main area of counter for food preparation. The stainless-steel pedestal legs allow space to sit or stand comfortably at any point around the perimeter of the island.

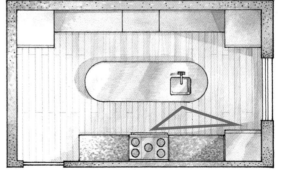

3

3 This island's configuration concentrates the work triangle between the cooktop, sink, and tall built-in refrigerator. Counter space on either side of the cooktop can be used for placing pans and appliances.

4 The main function of the island is to provide a cool granite counter for food preparation, and below-counter storage for cook books, fresh fruit and vegetables, and wines where everything can be easily seen and accessed.

4

5

6

cross refer to :

activity areas 54

stovetop cooking 62

serving & eating 66

kitchen materials 84

5 Incorporating split-level surfaces within an island provides the ergonomic answer for accommodating a range of activities. Recessed and pull-out woven baskets enhance the eclectic nature of this country-style kitchen.

6 A large room is best if planning an island layout. Here, the range is set in the original chimneypiece, with the island located centrally. The sink and cabinets around the perimeter make a spacious and effective work triangle.

7 A central island for preparing food works well in this L-shaped family kitchen. The hardwearing beech countertop provides a practical work surface in the center of the room, a few steps away from the range and sink. Towels are hung on a rack at the end of the island, ready to wipe dry plates and glasses before they are put away in the storage cabinet below.

DESIGN POINTS

Create a visual link between the kitchen and living area by selecting a coordinating color scheme. Make sure that the furnishings can be easily steam-cleaned or removed for machine washing, since food, drink, and grubby hands will soil surfaces between linked kitchen/living areas.

An island requires electricity, plumbing, and gas supplies to be installed. Remember to allow access so that the utilities can be easily serviced and maintained.

Where the island forms part of a large living/dining area, it is important to make sure that there is adequate ventilation. Preventing odors, grease, and steam drifting beyond the cooktop and oven will keep furnishings from absorbing strong smells and grease.

7

Portable islands

There are several reasons why portable islands are more practical than built-in designs: portable units are easily moved around the room; they will turn on their axis so that drawers and shelves can face in any direction; and cleaning the floor is quicker, as crumbs and spills are easy to reach. They are also less expensive than fitted ones.

Portable islands are particularly useful for smaller kitchens, since they provide additional counter space for food preparation, and can be stored under a counter after use or simply moved to one side to gain access to nearby cabinets or appliances.

Surfaces

The two most popular choices for portable islands are wood and stainless steel. Hardwoods, such as maple and beech, are often used for butcher's blocks, giving a resilient surface for cutting and chopping. The wood can absorb strong odors, so should be well cleaned after use. Stainless steel is a high-performance material that suits modern kitchen styles. It is heatproof, non-corrosive, hygienic, and washable.

cross refer to :
choosing a style 16
base cabinets 38
storing kitchenware 58
quick-fix changes 98

1 Two rectangular tables made from strong, lightweight stainless-steel panels are positioned centrally within reach of the sink. The units are constructed to a professional standard, incorporating a finish that is hygienic and easily cleaned. Pans and appliances occupy the shelving beneath, and open sides enable easy access.

4 This large island is used mainly for food preparation. A metal rail prevents heavy pans from sliding off the bottom shelf when the table is being moved around the kitchen.

2 In the style of a traditional butcher's block, this design incorporates a pull-out rack for fresh ingredients and a slatted base to hold large pans and accessories. The sturdy pull can double as a towel rail.

3 Chunky wheels, each fitted with a brake, increase the flexibility of this movable island that turns neatly on its axis. A polyurethane finish prevents moisture from damaging the interior of the wooden drawer.

ACTIVITY AREAS

Activity areas

Most kitchen activities revolve around the sink and food preparation and cooking areas. To maximize efficiency, position the activity zones within a short distance of each other so you can move effortlessly between them.

Depending on how much time you spend in the kitchen and how much cooking you do, certain appliances and features will be of greater importance than others. If the kitchen is intended as a room where meals are eaten and children can do homework or watch television, then you will need to define the areas so that activities do not conflict.

The sink area gets most use, whether it is for soaking dishes, rinsing fruit and vegetables, filling with pans, or garbage disposal, so it must be well planned. You should be able to move from the sink to the food preparation area easily. The refrigerator will be used by all the family as cold drinks, milk for cereals, coffee and tea, and snacks are always in demand. Place it toward the entrance to the kitchen to avoid people cutting across the cooking and sink areas to reach it. If space permits, include refrigerated drawers beneath the food preparation area for access to chilled ingredients.

Items within reach

Bear in mind the nature of each activity area to ensure optimum success. For example, fresh food storage should be planned away from hot, steamy areas of the kitchen, with separate, airtight containers for dry goods. Narrow shelves and pull-out drawers help to keep food items within reach and ensure that they are used before they deteriorate. Long-life foods can be fitted into less accessible storage areas. Store knives and cooking utensils close to the area where they will be needed. Herbs and spices should also be kept within close range of the food preparation area.

Moving between areas

Plan the different activity areas so that you progress naturally from the refrigerator to the sink, then to the food preparation area and finally to the stove. For safety, it is important to keep certain areas free of extraneous traffic. The stove, oven, or range are potentially hazardous as hot pans and dishes are moved into and out of them. To avoid crossing other activity areas where children may be occupied, make sure that there is an adjacent area of countertop on which to place hot dishes as soon as they have been removed from the stove or oven.

1 Plan the kitchen activity areas to follow the natural preparation stages for cooking. Keep cooking equipment, knives, and utensils close to where they are most used.

2 In the busiest activity area in the kitchen, a double sink provides a basin for cleaning fish, fruit, or vegetables with a second basin left free for dirty dishes.

3 Organize storage for flatware, plates, glasses, and linens so the table can be set without having to cross other activity areas.

4 Keep sharp knives in shallow drawers with narrow compartments. Knives will be quicker to locate, and will maintain sharper blades than they would if allowed to knock against each other.

5 A dresser unit offers open shelving and drawers so you can see, at a glance, items for setting the table.

6 If space allows, keep fruit and vegetables in chiller drawers beneath the food preparation area. If you have a compost bin, include a container nearby for vegetable waste.

1

2

3

cross refer to

ovens 72

cooktops & hoods 74

sinks & faucets 78

lighting 88

5

6

DESIGN POINTS

◢ If your family and guests like to join in with preparing meals, plan a small secondary sink and chopping area where they can work safely away from the stovetop or range.

◢ Ascertain how easy it is for more than one cabinet or appliance door to be open at one time and, if necessary, look at sliding or two-way opening options, or reverse hinges which are available on some appliances.

◢ As a lot of time in the kitchen is spent rinsing ingredients and washing-up, place the sink so that it faces either a window allowing for natural daylight and a good view, or into the room so that the user does not have to face a blank wall. If the sink faces into the room, conversation with guests is easier or the television can be watched.

4

Food storage areas

How you shop, how often you cook, the type of foods you use, and the number of people for whom you regularly provide meals – all of these variables have a bearing on the type and extent of food storage that best suits you.

Shelves piled high with cans and jars, or fresh foods deteriorating before you use them, are a good indication that your kitchen storage is in need of reorganization. To work out the most suitable system, start by dividing your food storage needs into two categories: perishable and non-perishable foods.

Perishable foods

Fresh, chilled, and frozen foods can only be kept for a short time before they begin to deteriorate. Bread and cakes need to be stored in airtight containers, while fruit and vegetables are best kept in a cool, well-ventilated area of the kitchen. Avoid filling the refrigerator with bottles, jars, or cans that could just as easily be stored elsewhere. Chiller drawers beneath the countertop are a practical addition for easy access

during food preparation. Look for a deep-freezer with several tray sizes so that both large and small items can be quickly located.

Non-perishable foods

Store non-perishable foods in pull-out pantry units, on shelves, or in leftover kitchen spaces. Keep everything accessible with dividers, racks, pull-out grids, and containers, grouping similar products and ingredients together.

Practical considerations

Storage areas are most accessible between eye level and knee height. For safe, easy removal, place heavier products below waist level and lighter items above. Where items are stored on narrow shelves, look for gallery units and mid-height rails to prevent items from falling off shelves.

1 Slim, pull-out pantry cabinets make efficient use of narrow spaces. Open sides ensure that all stored products can be quickly found. Place heavier items in the base compartment so that they can be removed safely.

2 Vegetables stay fresh if they are stored in well-ventilated containers, such as these wooden-framed, mesh drawers, installed beneath the food preparation area.

3 In island kitchens or a secondary preparation area, a supplementary refrigeration unit can be useful. Refrigerator or deep-freezer drawers can fit almost anywhere, allowing produce to be stored where it is most frequently used.

cross refer to

wall cabinets 36

base cabinets 38

activity areas 54

refrigerators 76

5 Walk-in pantries are a possible option, or a full-height storage cabinet offers a useful alternative. Its large capacity holds fresh and non-perishable foods in a variety of shelves and drawers, keeping everything in one easily accessible place. Choose a cabinet with removable fittings so they can be cleaned when necessary.

6 A freestanding pantry unit adds visual interest to this kitchen. A range of different shelf sizes allow all the contents to be stored at a convenient height where they can be clearly seen.

4

4 As chilled and frozen foods need to be put in the refrigerator or deep-freezer soon after you get in from shopping, make sure that there is a surface nearby where other heavy bags can be placed while unpacking.

Front vents allow a refrigerator or deep-freezer to be fitted flush with the wall, minimizing the accumulation of dust behind the unit.

DESIGN POINTS

Make sure that shelf heights and cabinet interiors can be adjusted to accommodate large boxes of cereal and tall bottles, as well as small cans, jars, and packages.

Interesting dried ingredients and bottles of preserves add esthetic appeal to kitchens, but steam and grime can build up on their surface, causing deterioration. Use and replace them regularly or, if you keep them just for show, wipe them occasionally to maintain their appearance.

Some foods, such as cookies, cakes, and pastries, are better stored at room temperature. Keep them covered and place them in a well-ventilated drawer or kitchen cabinet.

Regularly go through the cabinet to check "use before" dates. Place older items to the front so that they will be consumed first.

6

Storing kitchenware

Most kitchens contain a variety of cookware; plan storage so those items used every day are given prime storage space. Store special equipment, such as cake pans, where they will not obstruct access to frequently used pieces.

Prime storage space is the most easily accessed – usually somewhere between knee and eye level. Pans, large dishes, and utensils that you use at least once a day should be stored on shelving that does not necessitate stretching up or bending down to remove. Place large and heavy pans in cabinetry beneath countertops where lifting will not be a problem.

Access to corner cabinets is notoriously awkward, but pull-out fittings and Lazy-Susans allow the contents to be easily seen and selected. Special finishes, such as non-stick coatings, ridged skillets, and copper, can be damaged if pans are stacked on top of each other. Instead store them on their sides in pan-racks fitted in deep shelves.

efficiently, keeping items visible but unobtrusive. As with all activity areas, store everyday items within easy reach so that it is possible to work with the minimum of effort.

A practical solution to keeping an attractive display visible while reducing the need for regular cleaning, is to choose one or two sections of wall cabinetry fitted with clear or opaque glass fronts. Individual compartments give a sense of order to decorative as well as functional items; their big advantage is that they prevent items knocking against each other and items can be removed without lifting other pieces out of the way. However, they are more expensive than shelving and are not as adaptable.

1 Utilize every inch of space by paying particular attention to awkward areas. This two-part, pull-out, unit houses everyday items at the front, while special equipment at the back is reached once the front section is opened to the side.

2 Space above head height is often underused. A hanging rack or shelves provide room for pans, utensils, or seasonings to be suspended above the food preparation area or island.

3 Heavy, cumbersome pans need to be placed in sturdy drawers with smooth runners. The shallow drawer sides make lifting and removing pans easier.

Displaying or hiding items

The patina of copper pans and the gleam of stainless steel utensils look simple and efficient and add an eclectic element to kitchen decor – but choose what you show with care, and keep chipped, worn, and stained kitchenware out of sight. Whatever you choose to display, make sure that it is regularly cleaned as dust and grease will soon dull the finish.

Easy access

The key to accessible storage is to plan the width and height of fittings so that items are organized and quick to find. Simple solutions are often the best: for example, a compact knife block, wallmounted magnetic knife holder, or utensils . hanging from a rack suspended over the food preparation area all function

DESIGN POINTS

▤ When suspending pans from a hanging rack, choose a design with a grid shelf above or set aside a separate cabinet drawer below to store the corresponding lids.

▤ Choose a series of graduated drawers beneath the stove to store pans, utensils, knives, oven mittens, and trivets that are needed while cooking.

▥ It is surprising how even clean pans can mark shelves when they are put away. Choose a laminate or other washable finish that can be cleaned quickly and easily.

▥ Use thick shelf and drawer liners for dishes and glassware as they will absorb knocks and can be replaced once they become greasy or grimy.

cross refer to
wall cabinets 36
base cabinets 38
activity areas 54
cabinet finishes 94

4 A large, full-height cabinet has greater storage capacity than the base and wall cabinets where a gap for a countertop is left between them.

A Small display compartments offer individual storage options for collectables.

B Metal shelving is adjustable, strong, and removable for easy cleaning, and allows light to filter into every dark corner.

C A raised front edge or lip prevents jars from being inadvertently knocked off shelves.

D The large counter space is useful for placing dishes before taking them to the table and accommodates baskets of fruit or bread for everyday use.

E Opaque sliding doors semi-conceal disorderly piles of plates and other equipment.

F These drawers are finished with glass inserts to echo the style of the doors, allowing light to enter and illuminate the contents.

Chopping, rinsing, & mixing

Everyday food preparation tasks require well-planned areas where access to the sink is quick and easy, allowing several activities to be in progress at the same time. Choose a durable countertop with either an integral or separate chopping block that is tough enough to take the heaviest wear.

Allow a long, clear area of counter for chopping, mixing, and other food preparation tasks. Plan the stretch of counter so the sink is toward one end and the stove toward the other. Do not cram the appliances to the farthest edges as this will restrict your movement when using them; allow space at either end so that hot pans can be placed down next to the stove and dishes can be drained to one side of the sink.

Whether you prefer a solid wood surface for chopping everything or a series of dense, color-coded plastic boards for preparing different ingredients, make sure that they can be stored on or near the counter and that they can be easily cleaned, without joins or seals to trap dirt.

Professional standards

Enthusiastic cooks who spend a lot of time in the kitchen will want the highest quality equipment to deal with a wide range of preparation tasks. It is important to plan efficient storage so that equipment does not clutter the chopping, rinsing, and mixing areas when not in use.

Consider the advantages of a built-in marble slab for rolling pastry and a butcher's block for chopping and slicing. Making them an integral part of the countertop eliminates the need for separate boards. Stainless steel is a hygienic, durable, and multipurpose material and the choice for professional and contemporary kitchens. It can be used for a full-length, seamless counter, with sink, draining board, and backsplash, that is easy to clean after use.

1 At waist height, this original butcher's block offers the best ergonomic height for chopping. Its endgrain construction wears well, keeping knife blades sharp and stopping them from slipping when they make contact.

DESIGN POINTS

⬛ Plan the chopping, slicing, and mixing area between the sink and stove so rinsed ingredients can be drained, prepared, and transferred to the stove.

⬛ For safety and convenience, plan the lighting so that the sink, counter, and stove have shadowless light. Choose undercabinet lighting where possible.

⬛ Utilize the backsplash by fitting shallow shelving or a wall grid storage system where small utensils can be kept.

2 Appliance garages make full use of the space between wall and base cabinets to store miscellaneous items that are needed frequently. To allow appliances to be used from a set position, incorporate at least one electrical outlet inside the garage.

cross refer to
activity areas 54
sinks & faucets 78
waste & recycling 82
countertops 92

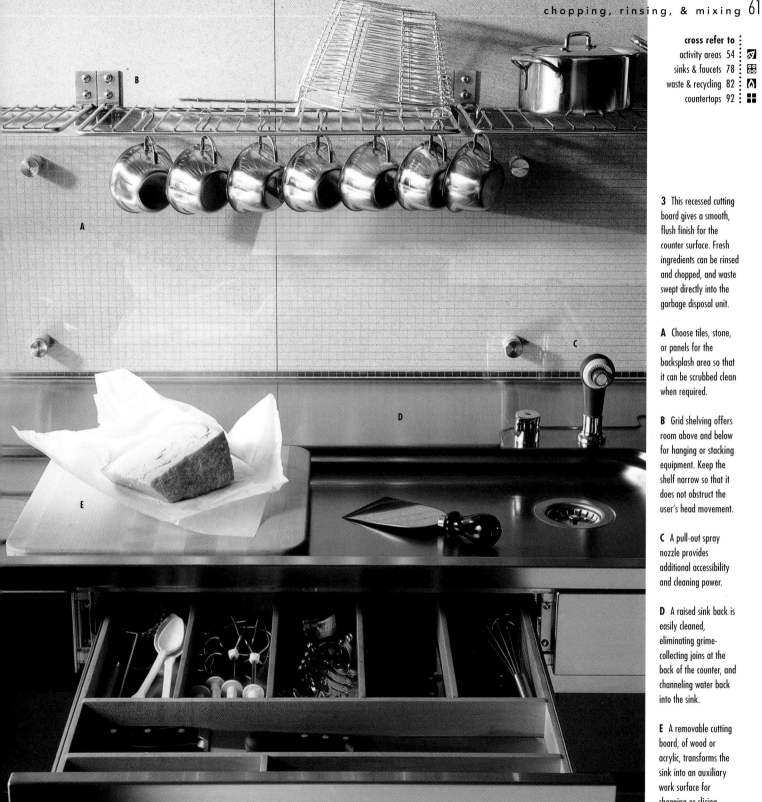

3 This recessed cutting board gives a smooth, flush finish for the counter surface. Fresh ingredients can be rinsed and chopped, and waste swept directly into the garbage disposal unit.

A Choose tiles, stone, or panels for the backsplash area so that it can be scrubbed clean when required.

B Grid shelving offers room above and below for hanging or stacking equipment. Keep the shelf narrow so that it does not obstruct the user's head movement.

C A pull-out spray nozzle provides additional accessibility and cleaning power.

D A raised sink back is easily cleaned, eliminating grime-collecting joins at the back of the counter, and channeling water back into the sink.

E A removable cutting board, of wood or acrylic, transforms the sink into an auxiliary work surface for chopping or slicing.

Stovetop cooking

A stovetop has to cope with a range of cooking methods, from fast frying to gentle simmering, as well as with small and large pans. Plan its position within reach of the sink and at a height that allows you to see clearly into pans.

1 Condensation and steam can be a problem in kitchens. Install a ventilation system that will cope with the amount of steam generated and that runs quietly enough for normal conversation levels to be heard.

Planning the kitchen so that the stovetop is positioned on an exterior wall is the most practical, if uninspiring, choice. Where the kitchen cabinetry fits around the perimeter of a kitchen, such as in a one-wall galley or an L- or U-shaped layout, it is impossible to plan the stovetop to face into the kitchen. However, peninsula and island units make it possible to site the stovetop so that it faces into the room rather than toward a blank wall.

Some models offer a pan-rest area or plate-warming section; otherwise you will need to allow space next to the stove for placing hot pans. Make sure that the surrounding surface can withstand the intense heat, or keep two or three pot stands at the side. Alternatively, incorporate a heat-resistant insert into the countertop where pans can be left.

Ideal stovetop height

The ideal height for a stovetop is just below waist level so that pans at the back can be reached and lifted without putting a strain on your back. The result is that it is likely to be lower than the surrounding counter, so you will need to make sure that the sides of cabinets are protected from steam, splashes, and grease.

Stovetops positioned at a low level should have surface-mounted controls that are clearly visible from a standing position. Backsplash and counter areas adjacent to the stovetop will have to be hardwearing, so choose a surface with a smooth, seam-free finish that can be scrubbed clean when necessary.

Fresh & bright

Steam, dust, and grime soon build up on kitchen equipment and surfaces, giving everything a dingy patina. A good ventilation system is essential to keep the air fresh and clean. Aim to get a fan powerful enough to remove fumes with the minimum of noise disruption. When buying, remember to check the cfm (cubic feet per minute) and sones. The cfm rating expresses the volume of air the unit can vent, and the sones measure the sound it emits: the lower the number, the quieter the fan – usually between 4.5 and 7 sones.

DESIGN POINTS

To make sure that there is sufficient light to work by, ventilation hoods with built-in lights combine two useful features in one unit.

Work out the ideal height for the stovetop by situating it 4–7in (10–17.5cm) below elbow level.

If you use cast-iron pans, look for a stovetop with a continuous grate across the top, making it easier to slide pots from one area of the stove to the next.

Choose a slim, pull-out ventilation hood that can be recessed beneath a wall fitting when not in use.

Island cook centers require a ventilation system that is powerful enough to draw up the air and carry it across the room before being vented to the outside. The farther the distance the air has to travel, the more the system's efficiency is reduced. Industrial designs for professional kitchens work best.

2

3

2 Raised edges around the stovetop contain pans within the designated area and prevent splashes of food and grease from penetrating the surrounding cabinetry.

3 Modular stovetop units are placed on either side of a large circular griddle – useful for searing meat and vegetables. The large, powerful ventilation hood spans the length of the worktop module to remove cooking fumes and grease quickly and efficiently.

4 This oven, stovetop, and ventilation configuration, with pan rests between the burners, makes the most of available space.

A Concealed ventilator vents are easily reached for maintenance.

B Opaque glass-fronted shelving keeps cooking equipment close to the stovetop but out of view.

C Task lights beneath the hood illuminate the area and allow clear visibility into pans.

D An adjustable plate rack near the stovetop allows plates to be warmed ready for use.

E Wallmounted dispensers simplify the task of cutting wrap and foil to length.

F A ventilator behind the stovetop provides fast, quiet extraction.

G A surface next to the stovetop area provides useful extra workspace when cooking.

H The sink is situated close to the stovetop so heavy pans can be easily moved to soak after use.

Oven cooking

Buying the oven and stovetop separately offers the perfect opportunity to combine appliances with the type of fuel and features you most prefer cooking with. Traditional ranges combine the oven and stovetop, with some offering a dual-fuel option.

There are two basic oven options: wall ovens and slide-ins, which fit under the counter. Under-counter ovens can be installed beneath the stovetop or located elsewhere so that movement around the two does not conflict. Combination microwave ovens built in with a single oven provide speed as well as the benefits of a convection oven and broiler.

Range-style cookers mostly run on natural or propane gas, electricity, or a combination of both. Fuels such as oil or solid fuel used in Agas, are less popular but Agas can be linked to the domestic heating system. Consider the cooking you do and choose a range to suit your needs.

Cooking for a family

Capacity and flexibility will be the main factors influencing your choice of oven if you cook for a family. Double ovens allow several dishes requiring varying temperatures and cooking times to be prepared together. Professional quality ranges are expensive and space consuming, but they have powerful burners and large-capacity ovens.

Busy people

If you are out at work most of the day, a delayed-time cooking facility will enable a meal to be ready on your return. Combination microwaves, which fast-cook, brown, and broil, are useful if you have irregular times for arriving home. Self-cleaning and continuous clean facilities are invaluable if you do not have the time or inclination to tackle the inside of the oven regularly.

Helpful additions

Do not buy an oven or range on its looks alone: assess your needs and look for designs that include some of the features you know will be useful.

Stay-cool fronts protect arms and hands from the intense heat inside. Electronic ignition is more efficient than a pilot light, which wastes fuel and can go out. Touchpad controls, activated by fingertip pressure, are useful for the less able. Dual-element ovens alternate between top and bottom elements for even heating. Convection ovens circulate hot air through the oven so foods cook and brown evenly. Steam circulation ovens keep meat moist without added fat and maintain moisture in foods yet they can still give breads and pizza a desirable crispy crust.

DESIGN POINTS

⊞ Drop-down doors are useful for placing hot dishes on once they have been removed from the oven.

⊞ Avoid fussy detailing. The fewer knobs, seams, and crevices there are, the less places grease and spills can collect.

🔥 Check oven capacities, as insulation for built-in and self-cleaning models can reduce the usable space inside.

🔥 Digital temperature displays enable you to check the oven temperature and pick up any variation. Oven preheating indicators show when the preset oven temperature has been reached.

🔧 If you are planning to install an Aga or a range, make sure that the floor can carry the weight of the appliance.

1

2

3

1 A combination built-in oven with halogen stovetop offers a compact cooking zone. The drop-down oven door provides a temporary shelf to place hot dishes and the ceramic-glass surface doubles as a countertop.

2 Large ranges are useful for families and professional cooks. Here, the stovetop lid opens to provide a practical backsplash, and the ventilation hood is powerful enough to remove the steam and fumes created by the various functions.

3 Combining stovetop and oven, standard ranges are easier to install than built-in options. The controls are easy to use, and an interior oven light allows you to monitor cooking as it progresses.

cross refer to
activity areas 54
ovens 72
cooktops & hoods 74
lighting 88

4 Cast-iron ranges, such as the Aga, are expensive but last a lifetime. They operate 24 hours a day and provide a choice of cooking methods in addition to heating for the home.

5 Instead of two conventional ovens, consider installing a combination microwave with the main oven. It frees up available counter space and, in addition to cooking food quickly, will brown and crisp effectively.

6 Double ovens can be used independently or together, depending on the quantity and type of food being cooked. When positioned at waist level, dishes are easy to lift in and out, and eye-level controls are easy to operate.

7 Combination microwaves set into a cabinet below the countertop are often sufficient for those who rarely cook. Facilities such as a turntable, heat sensor, and interior light help to produce meals that are thoroughly cooked and appetizing.

Serving & eating

Kitchens that also function as a place for eating will always be busy as people naturally congregate there. Plan the eating area so that it is practical and comfortable but does not restrict movement in the food preparation and cooking zones.

When choosing a table and seating for your kitchen, keep it simple. Chairs should be easy to wipe down and the table or countertop durable enough to withstand the inevitable accidents. Tables and chairs with splayed legs can be hazardous in small kitchens: pedestal tables, bench seats, and banquettes eliminate the problem and have the additional benefit of allowing several people to be squeezed in for impromptu meals. Folding and stacking chairs are easy to store away when extra space is needed.

Choosing the best view

Depending on whether or not you like people to watch as you cook, you may decide to partly screen the eating area from the kitchen. If the table faces a blank wall, people will automatically turn to something more interesting. A glass-fronted cabinet with a display of glassware, a large print or several of the children's paintings will all serve as a focal point. French doors or a large window can be opened to extend the view during warm weather and, in winter, strategic garden lighting will illuminate plants and special features.

The hub of the home

Sharing the kitchen with family and friends is one of the most enjoyable way of socializing but you will need to plan it so you can cook and carry on a conversation. A breakfast bar or island is ideal as a secondary food preparation area and, with high stools alongside, friends can perch while they join in the activities.

Warmth & light

Heat in the kitchen can be heavenly on cold days but stifling when the weather is hot. Plan the position of the breakfast counter or table so that it is at a comfortable distance from the cooking zone. A separate radiator nearby can boost the heat when required. In summer, a room fan provides a cooling breeze.

Kitchen activities need good task lighting so that jobs can be done safely and efficiently. However this can conflict with the softer, ambient light that is desirable for the eating area, so plan a flexible lighting scheme that can be altered to suit different occasions.

1 Utilize counter space along the wall of a galley kitchen by increasing the depth to accommodate high stools, creating an eating area. Padded seats and foot rests make these comfortable and relaxing to use.

2 An island with breakfast bar combines storage, preparation, and eating areas in one compact but accessible space. High stools face into the kitchen so other people can help without causing an obstruction.

3 A large kitchen room in a barn conversion is divided into two distinct halves by an open hearth. Food is prepared on a split-level island and then carried to the table for informal meals with family and friends.

4 Round tables allow free movement around the perimeter of the kitchen without obstruction from table corners. Small round tables will seat four comfortably, or six when the need arises.

5 Small kitchens can rarely accommodate a permanent table and chairs, so a foldaway design provides an inexpensive solution for informal meals. Folding or stacking chairs that can be stored away will use less floor space.

4

Kitchen furniture

Not every kitchen has room for a separate table and chairs, but it is surprising how flexible seating arrangements can be if you choose folding and stacking options that are brought out once the meal is ready. A slim breakfast bar with an appliance garage at the back doubles as a food preparation and eating area. It enables appliances to be stored out of sight when not in use, leaving the counter free for serving and eating.

Chair and table heights may be unsuitable for young children and babies. Make sure that you provide a high-chair that gives them the opportunity to see and learn from older children and adults.

cross refer to

island kitchens 50
kitchen materials 84
lighting 88
countertops 92

6 This round table has sturdy metal legs and a durable wooden surface so spills and splashes are easy to wipe away. It folds flat after use and can be stored in a kitchen cabinet which makes it a good choice for small rooms.

7 Choose an area of the kitchen away from the heat and noise for entertaining. Although not totally separate, the dining table provides a safe area for younger family members to sit where the cook is able to keep a watchful eye on their activity.

6

DESIGN POINTS

For additional comfort, washable seat covers are ideal and add color to plain schemes. Make sure that they have ties to secure them to the seat or they will tend to fall onto the floor each time the occupant moves or stands.

High stools use up less space than chairs but can become uncomfortable after a while, so look for designs that offer foot rests and back supports.

Choose a surface with rounded edging for countertop eating as it will eliminate hard, angled edges that can hurt if knocked against.

Provide heat-resistant mats on which to place hot pans if they will be transferred straight from the stovetop to serve at the table.

Plan a cabinet close to the eating area for glasses, plates, and cutlery.

5

7

Storing utility items

Where space is limited it is not always possible to have a separate utility room for laundry appliances and cleaning equipment. If this is the case, group items in close proximity to create a well-organized area away from the food preparation zone.

Stacking appliances and combined washer/dryers are ideal for compact kitchens, but the noise of a spin cycle can be disruptive. If space permits, a dividing screen or folding door will shut off the laundry area when necessary. Include a tall cabinet to accommodate larger pieces of equipment such as the ironing board, vacuum, and broom. Organize the internal fittings so that everything is secured and will not tumble forward when the door is opened.

Planning the space

For reasons of hygiene, position washers and dryers away from food preparation and cooking areas. Plan their location beyond the main work triangle and toward the end of a run of cabinets. Appliances requiring plumbing are best situated along one wall, with storage for household chemicals and cleaning equipment nearby. Consider fitting a cabinet for these items between the laundry equipment and the sink so they can be easily reached from either side.

Unless you have a condenser-dryer, good ventilation is required to remove moisture from damp laundry. Site the drier against an exterior wall so that ducting is minimal and the water vapor can escape into the outside air. Steam can be a problem if it rises and condenses on porous surfaces, so choose a counter that will not swell or warp in damp conditions. Maintain a slight gap around washing machines and washer/dryers to prevent appliances vibrating against adjacent cabinets.

1 The washer is situated to take advantage of the existing plumbing without crossing into the main work triangle. The integrating door blends in with the surrounding cabinet fronts.

2 Storage within this tall cabinet has been divided to accommodate the length of the vacuum cleaner hose, ironing board, brooms, mops, and other cleaning epuipmemt, while chemicals and cloths are stacked on pull-out shelving.

cross refer to
design your kitchen 34
base cabinets 38
washing machines 81

DESIGN POINTS

▤ Even if children rarely visit you, make sure that dangerous chemicals are kept on high shelves – completely out of reach from little hands.

▦ Add cabinet fronts to appliances so that they blend with surrounding units.

1

2

EQUIPMENT

Selecting equipment

Well-designed equipment is the linchpin of an efficient kitchen. To help make your choices, consider how easy appliances are to operate, the differences in fuel consumption and the durability of the materials used in their construction.

2 For a compact kitchen, this freestanding unit combines storage, rinsing and food preparation areas with tough stainless steel and wood finishes that are easy to keep clean.

3 Temperature and cleaning options offer greater control of washing and drying cycles while conserving water and energy.

It may be tempting, in an effort to keep costs down, to consider using existing equipment in your new kitchen but, unless it is less than five years old, it could be a false economy. Innovative new products with improved materials, safety features, and greater energy efficiency will not only give better results but can save money in the long term.

Assess your needs and look for products that offer the facilities you are most likely to use. Designs that save time, money, and effort, such as delay-time dishwashers that make use of off-peak electricity, can be a real asset. Check all measurements, capacities, color choices, and price guides to make sure that you end up with the right design for you. Buy the best you can afford and, if necessary, wait until you see the product on sale or in a discount store.

Energy issues

Global warming and the unrelenting consumption of the Earth's natural resources have highlighted the need for fuel efficiency. Recent innovations have produced a wide range of goods that are either constructed from recycled materials or are inherently recyclable. Initially, buying a sturdy, well-designed product will be more expensive, but you can expect it to perform well and last far longer than a cheaper one.

Refrigerators must now comply with the international ban on chlorofluorocarbon refrigerants (CFCs), which damage the Earth's protective ozone layer. The latest models use hydrofluorocarbons (HFCs), which work as efficiently but are more eco-friendly.

Improved insulation on new ovens and refrigerators, better seals, and fast-response controls all help to reduce the amount of energy consumed for the appliance to operate efficiently. Water consumption and biodegradable detergents that affect the quality of our water are factors that have influenced the latest designs in dishwashers. Redesigning the washing action and finding the optimum temperature to make sure that dishes are thoroughly cleaned

1 A large range with a choice of burners provides greater versatility for a cook who caters for several family members or guests at one time.

cross refer to
refrigerators 76
dishwashers 80
washing machines 81

4 Brushed stainless steel is practical for heavy duty areas and makes an eyecatching feature where several items are combined. The fast, efficient ventilator hood removes exhaust fumes quickly and also quietly.

5 Professional quality knives provide safe, accurate chopping, slicing, and peeling. Choose a knife that sits comfortably in your hand and is balanced.

6 This food mixer has a large capacity and a powerful motor to handle large quantities with ease. The bowl is fitted with a handle to make lifting and pouring easier.

7 Freestanding refrigerators, such as this, are a striking feature. Look for models that sit on wheels so that they can be moved easily to clean behind and for servicing. Ventilation at the front enables the unit to be fitted flush to the wall.

use. For example, do you need a set of four or five professional knives that will fillet fish or chop herbs effortlessly, or would you use a food mixer that will beat, whisk, and blend large and small quantities, more. Look for smooth, durable finishes that are easily cleaned. Avoid items with intricate detailing unless you have time to keep them grime-free. Maintain your equipment as recommended by the manufacturer and it will give lasting service.

4

DESIGN POINTS

▨ Ask about delivery times, warranties, and servicing so that you do not have an unacceptable wait when you need assistance. Check that controls are easy to see and operate.

▦ Make sure that the appliance has a large enough capacity for your needs.

▦ Look for finishes that will withstand constant use and washing and will not require special cleaning to maintain their appearance.

▦ Choose each piece of equipment on its own merits, not because the color or finish matches another piece. It is always possible to conceal appliances behind a cabinet front or to fit an integrating panel where available.

◖ Consider what small appliances can easily be stored away after use or if you can spare the space for them to be a permanent feature on the countertop.

have all but eliminated the need for a time-consuming prewashing program, with consequent savings in energy consumption.

Sound control

Noise levels in the home can be irritating so it makes sense to check how noisy appliances are in operation. Insulation on many new appliances has reduced noise to a more acceptable level but they can vary, so it is worth checking. Even though an appliance can function quietly, the vibration created while it is running can be intrusive.

Attention to detail

Good-quality utensils and appliances will improve the smooth running of every kitchen chore. Buy the best you can afford as they will give better results and last longer than cheaper alternatives. Pare your requirements down to what you really need and

5

7

Ovens

Once you have decided on the type of cooking equipment you need, consider the facilities each has to offer. Some manufacturers produce the same design features in gas and electric versions so you can select the model that suits you best.

If you are a serious cook, then an oven offering the latest features is likely to be well used; otherwise, keep to a simple, durable design that is easy to operate. No matter what oven or range you choose, make clear and concise controls your top priority. They must be easy to grip and turn, and each one should be easy to read and obvious which burner or facility it operates.

Ovens

Built-in wall ovens situated at eye level enable you to monitor the cooking in progress, but can use up the space that would otherwise make a useful worksurface. They require special oven-housing cabinets to support the weight, and ventilation to prevent heat from damaging the surrounding materials.

Slide-in ovens fit under the counter, leaving the area above clear for food preparation. If you have difficulty lifting dishes, choose a model with a drop-down door, which provides a midway shelf between the oven and counter. Self-clean oven linings reduce the time spent cleaning.

Ranges

Freestanding gas or electric ranges are suitable for installing between or at the end of a run of cabinets. Flat, ridge-free sides enable the appliance to be fitted flush between cabinets for a neat finish, but make sure that there is adequate insulation to prevent heat transfer. A raised edge around the top prevents spills from running down the sides. Gas is very fuel-efficient and gives the cook maximum control over temperature. The latest electric models are designed to be as efficient but still take slightly longer to heat up and cool down.

Microwave & steam ovens

If most of your meals are ready-made, then countertop or built-in microwave/convection ovens will be the best choice. The best results are from ovens offering a minimum of 800 Watts. Some models have browning elements and broilers.

Steam ovens are essentially built-in pressure cookers. Connected to the water supply and programed for a length of time, they prevent steam from escaping, which in turn raises the pressure and temperature inside. Food can be cooked quickly, with minimum loss of nutrients and color.

1 A built-in oven and broiler are useful for cooking in small quantities and for simple meals. The drop-down door doubles as a shelf on which to stand hot dishes, and simple controls are easy to see and operate.

2 Create a compact and efficient cooking zone by installing the oven and microwave in an oven-housing cabinet. The glass front panel and internal light allows cooking to be monitored without opening the oven, and the shallow warming drawer keeps plates warm without using oven space.

3 Double wall ovens are ideal for busy cooks and those with large families, since dishes requiring different cooking temperatures and times can be cooked simultaneously. A cooktop situated elsewhere allows two people to cook without being interrupted.

4 Slide-in ranges are available in gas, electric or dual-fuel (gas and electric) models and are designed to sit on the floor between cabinets. The control panel is situated beneath the cooktop to give a simpler, built-in look.

5 Steam ovens are costly to install but practical for low-fat diets, since food retains moisture, color, and nutrients. They work by cooking foods under pressure, which raises the temperature for faster cooking times.

6 The classic Aga will cook and heat the domestic hot water. Some models will also operate radiators. They have two large boil and simmer cast-iron plates, and hot and cool ovens that operate 24 hours a day. They are ideal for cooler climates, where keeping the kitchen warm and aired is essential.

DESIGN POINTS

▦ Make sure that the pans you will use are suitable for the type of gas or electric burner you choose.

▦ If you are considering a colored oven finish, consider whether it will coordinate with the surrounding kitchen color scheme and if you are likely to tire of the shade in a few years before the oven needs replacing.

▦ Automatic electric spark ignition/re-ignition will light burners when the knob is set at any position, and will re-light if it is extinguished, even on its lowest setting.

▦ Look for removable doors, broiler trays, shelves, burner bowls, and caps to enable thorough cleaning.

🔥 Make a note of the BTU's (British thermal units) of the gas ovens and ranges you are considering, since it illustrates the heat output. 9000 is usual, but choose one nearer 12000 if you cook in large quantities and often.

▦ Allow at least 9in (23cm) of counter to one side of the range and 15in (38cm) on the other side so that pan handles can be accommodated and movement is unrestricted. Choose heatproof surfaces to flank both sides.

5

7 Professional-quality ranges offer more capacity than standard ranges, and in heavy-duty stainless steel look and cook superbly. Although the price is higher, the burners are usually more powerful and will last a long time.

8 Commercial-style ranges offer larger burners and more of them — often six with a griddle. The BTU output is greater too, so if you install one, make sure that the ventilator hood is placed at the manufacturer's minimum recommended height to prevent heat damage and risk of fire.

cross refer to
stovetop cooking 62
cooktops & hoods 74
kitchen materials 84
changing wall finishes 102

6

7

8

Cooktops & hoods

As most cooking is done on the cooktop, it is important to select one that offers the fuel type, burner arrangement, and facilities you need. Whatever your choice, make sure that the ventilation is powerful enough to remove the fumes, steam, and grease.

1 A funneled hood channels air up toward the exhaust fan.

2 This sleek hood, with integral lights and variable speeds, slides out from beneath the wall cabinet for use, and is put away afterward.

If you want a gas cooktop, look for sealed burners so that when liquid boils over, it does not run beneath and extinguish the flame. One-piece drip trays are easy to remove to clean such spills. Burner grates are round, square, or continuous. Continuous designs allow pans to slide across without needing to be lifted. They also stop pans placed off-center from tipping over. Look for safety features such as automatic re-ignition and the Smart Flame facility, which reduces the temperature on grate fingers. Pilotless ignition, energy-saving and convenient, is replacing pilot lights.

Standard electric cooktops with exposed coil elements are usually the most economical option. These work well if you make sure that the pan bases fit the diameter of each burner.

Ceramic-glass electric cooktops with elements beneath the surface are sleek and easy to clean, but only pans with smooth, flat bases can be used on them. The elements fall into three categories: radiant burners with coiled ribbon elements that glow red when on; quick-response halogen burners that generate heat by means of a halogen bulb; and magnetic induction burners that create an electromagnetic field when contact is made between a magnetic pan (not made from aluminum) and the surface, which then heats up.

Modular or other cooktops with specific functions can be located separately or grouped to suit your needs. Recess barbecue, deep frier, and boiler elements give your counters a sleek finish. Wok-burners, pot-warmer plates, rotisserie, and griddle systems can take some of the cooking chores away from the main cooking zone if desired.

Hoods & vents

The two main types of ventilation systems are updraft and downdraft. Recirculating hoods that filter air and blow it back into the kitchen are available, but not very effective – use them as a last resort. Hoods channel cooking fumes up and out, so should be at least 6in (15cm) wider than the cooktop to capture steam, grease, and odors. Downdraft units are sunk into the unit beside the cooktop or into the wall behind it and draw stale air from around the cooktop. Where fan noise is intrusive, see if the motor can be located in an adjacent utility room or the basement. Remember, however, the fan's effectiveness may be reduced by long runs of ducting.

DESIGN POINTS

▣ Make sure the cooktop you buy has a smooth, crevice-free surround so that it is easy to clean and maintain.

◢ The higher the CFM- (cubic feet per minute) rating, the more powerful the hood. The rating should not be less than 150cfm for a standard cooktop, but barbecue/griddle and grill facilities, which generate more heat and smoke, require a higher rating.

▥ If you prefer country-style fittings, disguise industrial-looking hoods behind matching cabinetry.

▣ Look for hoods with wire-mesh filters that can be cleaned easily.

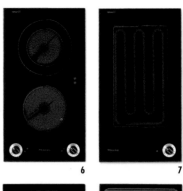

6 A ceramic double-burner has a small and large burner suitable for pans of matching size.

7 This broiler's electric element covers a large rectangular area within the module, to heat and brown food.

8 The electric deep frier is recessed to keep the countertop clear. It can be sealed with a cover to keep oil fresh when not in use.

9 Ideal as an indoor barbecue when the weather is bad, an electric grill is good for cooking fish, steaks, and kebabs any time.

cross refer to
island kitchens 50
activity areas 54
selecting equipment 70
lighting 88

3 Hoods for island use should be attractively finished on all sides like this striking glass and stainless steel design. Ducting has to travel up and across the room to be vented outside.

4 A large, smooth hot plate is ideal for searing meat and fish, and for making crêpes or griddle cakes. Position it where it benefits from the overhead exhaust hood: in a series of cooktops or alongside the main kitchen cooktop.

5 This hi-tech ceramic cooktop sits flush with the worktop for a neat, sleek finish. No ridges or seams mean the surface can be quickly and easily wiped clean after use.

10 The wok burner gives the intense and even heat required for stir-frying by supporting the shape of a wok.

11 This four-ring gas burner offers a range of flame intensities to suit all cooking needs and flame sizes for different pans. Removable grates are easy to clean.

12 The combination of four gas burners and a double electric ceramic burner meets a variety of cooking needs: ideal for cooks who regularly cater for large numbers.

13 The elements in this four-burner electric cooktop vary so that a range of pan sizes can be used. Energy is saved as only the elements required are heated.

Refrigerators

Refrigerators must be efficient to ensure food is kept at a low enough temperature to avoid deterioration. Choose one with a capacity that comfortably accommodates the foods you need to keep chilled and offers adaptable interior fittings for flexibility.

1 A commercial-style refrigerator keeps wines at an even temperature. Its glass door and shelves allow you to see inside.

2 This eye-catching model has a wide door base, allowing for storage of bulky items.

Appearances are important, but taking time to assess configuration, capacity, and ease of cleaning will pay dividends. A capacity of 6 cu ft (175 liters) is thought to be adequate for two people; add at least 1½ cu ft (42 liters) for each extra person. Other features to look for are an auto-defrost facility and ice- and chilled water dispensers. Check that the shelves can be adjusted to accommodate bottles and cans safely. Energy efficiency is also important: as well as using hydrofluorocarbon refrigerants, the latest models have improved door-seal insulation, cutting running costs.

Freestanding models

Slide-in or freestanding models can stand alone or in a convenient gap between cabinets. Front vents allow recent models to be recessed farther for more of a built-in look. Choose a model with wheels so that moving it for cleaning is easier.

Built-in choices

Generally wider and shallower than freestanding models, refrigerators that are built-in fit comfortably in standard-depth countertops. They tend to be more expensive, but can be finished to match the cabinetry. Good ventilation is essential to allow the heat produced to escape: make sure that they are fitted according to the manufacturer's guidelines. Do not site them next to a range or oven as the ambient heat will raise the temperature inside the refrigerator each time the door is opened, reducing fuel-efficiency.

3 This top-mount unit (freezer compartment is situated above the refrigerator) combines classic retro style with modern technology.

4 Modern refrigerators offer options such as a reversible door hinging for ease of access and an auto-defrost facility that eliminates the need for manual defrosting. They also display fuel-efficiency in the form of a kWh (kilowatt-hour) rating. Optimum for performance and economy is a rating around 0.65 kWh/24hr.

6

DESIGN POINTS

When measuring the refrigerator's dimensions, add enough to the width to allow the door to be opened fully.

Grid or glass shelving allows the internal lighting to filter through so that items stored at the back remain visible.

Built-in water filtration systems, icemakers and through-the-door water dispensers help keep the sink area free.

Store fruits, vegetables, and salad ingredients in drawers where they will be kept fresh and crisp and will not be damaged by too low a temperature.

Consider what configuration would best suit you: a side-by-side refrigerator/ freezer built-in beneath the countertop; or full length that allows you to store frequently-used items at eye-level. Top-mount refrigerators have a deep-freezer section above, bottom-mount have a pull-out section or a side-hinged door with deep-freezer drawers.

5 Built-in undercounter fridge-freezers keep the countertop free where space is limited. They are particularly useful if situated under the food preparation area as ingredients can be moved quickly into and out of both without the need to cross the kitchen when cooking or unpacking the groceries.

6 Drinking water and ice are available from this refrigerator door and inside, adjustable shelving accommodates a wide range of foods. Good internal lighting and transparent drawers ensure items are clearly visible. Front venting and a coil-free back allows the appliance to be set close to the wall.

7 Modular refrigerators such as these fit under the counter and make useful second chillers in any kitchen. They are good for those with special needs as the drawers slide smoothly.

8 Adjustable deep door shelves with high sides hold family-size bottles in place.

7

8

Sinks & faucets

The sink is one of the most frequently used items in the kitchen, so it must be both practical and durable. Consider who uses it, the size and type of items you wash, and make sure that sufficient space is allocated to install a suitable design.

1

The size of the sink is determined by the surrounding cabinet and countertop dimensions and your available budget. The position of the sink also needs careful consideration; if it is set too low or too high or set back too far in the base cabinet, then it is likely to cause back strain when used for long periods.

Simple, capacious sink designs are particularly useful for performing multiple tasks, especially when used in conjunction with an additional basin. Twin sinks simplify dishwashing and food rinsing functions even more. One can be used for rinsing greens while the other is used for filling with pans. Bowl-and-a-half sink units are also popular as they do not occupy a large amount of countertop space and cope adequately with general dishwashing and rinsing activities.

Sink materials

Stainless-steel sinks both look good and are durable, withstanding heat and household chemicals. Buy the best you can afford; ideally one constructed from an extra thick stainless steel and nickel. Enameled cast iron has seen a revival in recent years and is available in several colors. Although relatively inexpensive, beware of cheaper models as the enamel may chip. Porcelain-coated fireclay resists staining and heat damage but is heavy and needs mounting on a sturdy frame. An all-in-one solid surfacing material requires minimal maintenance and is easy to clean as there are no joins or ledges where dirt can accumulate. Composites are

made from stone such as granite or marble, bound in rosin. They are molded into shape and as the color runs through the material, stains and scratches can be easily removed.

Kitchen faucets

Choose spout and handle designs that are easy to operate and adapt to the cleaning or chores you undertake regularly. A solid, smooth finish retains its look while detailed designs trap dirt and grime. Where space is limited, opt for wallmounted fixtures to keep the countertop free. A pull-out spray nozzle is useful for filling pans and rinsing ingredients. Some spray faucets have an integral brush. Swan-neck or high arc designs allow room for large dishes in the sink. For double sinks, check that the faucet can swivel from left to right.

2

DESIGN POINTS

■ Make sure that the seals around the sink are watertight and kept in good condition to prevent water damage.

■ Consider installing a second small sink in the food preparation area for rinsing fresh ingredients.

■ If counter space is limited, choose a sink design where a chopping block can fit over the sink recess.

■ To keep the sink area clutter-free, choose a single-lever faucet that controls both water flow and temperature.

■ Sink designs where the waste outlet sits at the rear ensure pipework is kept at the back of the base cabinet, leaving space to store items at the front.

1 A round sink has less capacity than a square design with similar dimensions. Although its esthetic appeal makes it ideal as a secondary sink for light duties in modern kitchens.

2 Porcelain-coated fire clay offers a stain and heat-resistant surface for this traditional porcelain sink. Placed at the front of the counter, items can be lifted in and out with ease.

3 Some pans and delicate glassware are best washed by hand. A bowl-and-a-half sink is practical as it allows both washing and rinsing to be performed.

3

4 Corner sinks with two bowls set at a 90° angle make full use of the countertop space in the awkward corners of both L- and U-shaped rooms. Although economical with space, working in a tight corner can restrict the user's movement.

4

5

5 Draining boards can take up precious counter space when not in use. Consider those that fold or can be stored flat when not needed.

7

6 A fully-molded stainless-steel sink and draining board within this food preparation bench maintains a seamless work flow from right to left. Rinsed produce is left to drain in the shallow area while a large cutting board slides over the deep sink for chopping and slicing.

7 For light-duty rinsing, a small sink set into the food preparation area keeps the main sink clear for heavier duties and saves on trips across the kitchen.

8 Make sure that the faucet swivels easily to fill either bowl in a double sink. A high arc or swan-neck design allow space for oven trays and pans to be placed beneath the faucet for washing or filling.

6

8

Dishwashers

What is expected from a dishwasher will vary from one home to another, so choose features you know you will use. Above all, look for a reliable, energy-efficient design with user-friendly controls that simply do the dishes at the push of a button.

cross refer to
activity areas 54
serving & eating 66
selecting equipment 70

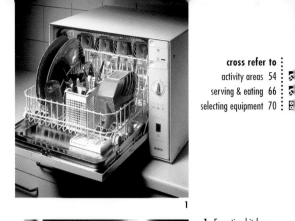

Technological and design innovations have greatly improved performance: the new breed of dishwasher holds more dishes, flatware, and odd-shaped items like bottles and baking pans than earlier models of the same size. The range of cleaning modes, water temperatures, and drying cycles means energy can be conserved and water consumption reduced; making dishwashers a viable alternative, both economically and environmentally, to washing the dishes by hand.

Features to choose

If you enjoy cooking and prepare meals for several people a day, the dishwasher capacity will need to be at least 12 settings. For couples or homes where most meals are ready-made, a countertop appliance will

suffice. High water temperatures and newly formulated detergents leave items exceptionally clean but may be too harsh for some cookware, so make sure that your dishes can tolerate them. A stainless-steel interior is best for durability, heat retention, resistance to odor absorption and chemicals. Sound insulation has improved too. Delay start buttons allow you to make use of off-peak electricity, or hold the program until the meal has finished.

Prime position

Aim to install the dishwasher close to the sink: this enables heavily soiled items to be rinsed before loading, and means that you can make use of existing plumbing, cutting installation costs. Allow enough space to open the door without restricting access to cabinets on the facing wall.

1 Even tiny kitchens will have room for a countertop dishwasher, which is compact and holds two place settings.

2 Many dishwashers are designed to take cabinet fronts to match the surrounding cabinets. Concealed controls in the top of the door are esthetically pleasing, and prevent small children from playing with the buttons.

3 Stainless steel is a high-quality, durable material and although expensive, withstands heavy use and harsh chemicals. With regular servicing, you can expect a stainless-steel unit to last for a minimum of 20 years.

4 Compact narrow dishwashers save space in small kitchens while still offering the facilities that larger models do.

DESIGN POINTS

Look for models offering at least two revolving spray-arm wash systems to make sure that water is forced between closely packed dishes, the prongs of forks and inside mugs.

Make sure that the model you buy has anti-flood sensors that cut off water the instant a leak is detected.

Convection-drying circulates air to remove moisture from the items inside so that they can be removed quickly for storing or re-use, but do check inside upturned articles for pools of water.

Regularly clean the filter and remove any particles clogging holes in the spray arms.

Washing machines & dryers

cross refer to
activity areas 54
selecting equipment 70
sinks & faucets 78
flooring 90

Your needs and the available space will determine what machine you buy. If you can, a washing machine with a separate tumble-dryer is a better option than a combined washer-dryer, although these do save space. Review washes, spin speeds, temperatures, and drying programs to make sure that you choose one that offers the best combination for you.

A utility area dedicated to washing, drying, and ironing is practical and keeps food preparation and laundry apart. With studio living and space restrictions this luxury is not always possible, so the two functions often take place side-by-side. If you can, install the washing machine near the door so dirty laundry is not carried through food preparation areas.

Amount of use

A combined washer-dryer will easily handle small amounts of washing, but many combined machines are only able to dry half the weight of the original wash load. If you do a minimum of one wash cycle a day, a separate dryer is useful, allowing a second load to be in the washing machine while the first dries.

A machine's dimensions are no indication of a washer's capacity. Front-loading or horizontal axis washers are smaller but have similar capacities to larger, top-loading machines. Top-loading machines require space for an agitator, while front-loading designs jostle the laundry through the water and do not require such a large drum.

Choosing a site

Site the washer close to the sink to use existing plumbing runs and keep installation costs down. A separate dryer should be placed on an outside wall so that the moisture-laden air can be ducted away efficiently, unless it is a condenser-dryer, which collects the moisture for emptying at the end of the program, or channels the moisture out through the waste pipe.

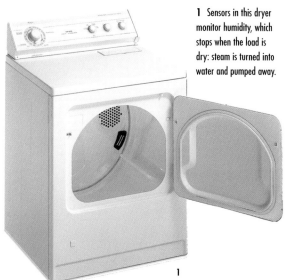

1 Sensors in this dryer monitor humidity, which stops when the load is dry: steam is turned into water and pumped away.

2 Front-loading washer-dryers are fitted beneath the countertop. They combine two functions so occupy less space.

3 The smooth surfaces of this machine provides a temporary shelf to stack laundry, while the top-mounted control panel is clearly visible.

4 Even though this top-loader is only 24in (61cm) wide, it can still accommodate full loads.

DESIGN POINTS

Front-loading machines are more efficient since they require less water and detergent to wash a load and are consequently cheaper to run.

Unlike front-loading machines, top-loading models can be opened after the program has started to allow a forgotten item to be dropped in.

Make sure that your machine has either self-leveling or adjustable feet to compensate for uneven floors, which may affect performance and wear.

Highly absorbent items such as towels, comforters, and pillows can cause washing loads to become unbalanced, making agitation during washing and drying less efficient. Look for self-balancing machine tubs that detect and correct imbalances automatically.

Waste & recycling

We are all aware of the importance of responsible waste-disposal, so plan a system that every family member can use easily. Decide what can be recycled, if you have space for composting vegetable matter and how much will still end up in the garbage.

cross refer to
activity areas 54
chopping & rinsing 60
selecting equipment 70

1

Evaluate the recycling possibilities open to you by finding out from your local authority what facilities exist. Check also whether you can install a food-waste disposal to reduce the amount in every garbage collection.

Trash compactors compress and minimize the volume of organic, synthetic, and other waste products that you cannot recycle.

Organic waste

Either throw organic waste away with general household trash, grind it in a waste-disposal, or compost it for use in the garden. Sort garbage at source by keeping a container for organic matter next to the sink or have a waste hole cut in the countertop so peelings are scraped into it.

2

DESIGN POINTS

⚠ If your home has a septic tank, waste-disposal is not recommended; too much material washed down can make the septic tank ineffective.

▤ Only compost vegetable waste since bread, meat, eggs, and fish will smell bad and attract unwanted pests, such as flies and rodents.

▦ There are two types of waste disposal: in the first, a batch feed, a chamber is filled with waste and water, covered with a locking lid, and it grinds a single batch at a time. The second disposal is continuous feed. Water is run in as the unit is switched on and food waste is fed into the chamber.

1 A deep drawer that is compartmentalized for recyclable materials keeps the kitchen free of clutter. If you have space, choose large garbage bins to store several days' waste.

2 If you prepare a lot of vegetables and fresh fruit, a waste hole in the counter makes disposing of peelings easy and hygienic. The drawer below has a washable liner to keep it fresh.

3 These swing-top garbage bins will sit neatly beneath the counter or at the end of cabinets without using valuable floor space.

4 Compactors compress everything down to a minimum, saving space and reducing trips to the trash can outside. Larger models compress more but the bundles may be heavy to lift. Some have charcoal filter systems to remove odors.

5 A recycling bin on wheels and divided into compartments can be moved to the food preparation area, sink or table so that waste is placed inside with ease.

3   4   5

SURFACES & FINISHES

Kitchen materials

Surface materials are available in an infinite range of colors, patterns, and textures, so make sure that you consider key factors such as the material's location, durability, and cost of installation to find the most suitable materials for your kitchen.

Heat, steam, knocks, household chemicals, and abrasive cleaners soon take their toll on inferior products so it is important to find out as much as you can about the properties of each material: how durable it is and how it changes over time. Start by looking at each surface in turn: flooring, cabinetry, countertops, backsplash, walls, and even furniture. Assess the advantages and disadvantages of each and compile a list of features that could have a bearing on your decision such as whether there are young children or pets to consider, how much cooking you do, and how easy each surface is to maintain.

1 Laminated surfaces such as this countertop resist abrasion, stains, and moisture but sharp knives and hot pans can damage the surface.

Wood

Widely used for floors, cabinets, and countertops, wood mellows and in time develops a patina. Hardwoods are more expensive and durable than softwoods, which are easily scratched and dented. Wood veneers have a uniform grain and color but may chip. Heat, humidity, or very dry conditions can cause wood to split and warp.

Laminate

Used for floorings, countertops, cabinets, and wall paneling, laminate finishes include wood, stone, and tile effects, as well as contemporary, plain, or patterned designs. High-pressure laminates are more durable, but correspondingly more expensive, than the low-pressure laminates.

Glass & ceramic

Ceramic tiles are heat-resistant, hardwearing, waterproof, and easy to clean. They are suitable for walls, countertops, and flooring, but the grout between them will not wear as well and discolors easily as dirt and grime collects in the joins. Glass maintains a feeling of space and airiness, and is especially useful for small kitchens, and ideal for contemporary style. It is a good choice for cabinet fronts, backsplash,

2 Terra-cotta's natural texture and subtle tones add warmth to kitchen schemes. Terra-cotta floor tiles are hardwearing and soft underfoot but as they are porous, must be sealed to prevent moisture penetrating and staining.

2

1

3 Wood flooring is easy to keep clean, warm underfoot, and hygienic. It is available in a wide range of natural grains and tones as well as colored stains. Heavy items may dent the boards if dropped, and heat and moisture can cause wood to warp.

3

4 Specially formulated kitchen paints resist moisture and grease penetration and contain fungicides to inhibit mildew growth. The surface is easily wiped clean and tolerates scrubbing to remove stubborn marks.

5 Bold paint colors make a strong design statement and are the easiest, least expensive, and quickest way of transforming walls and changing the character of a kitchen room. Laminate cabinets absorb light to give the interior a contemporary plain matte finish.

4

and, when frosted, creates an attractive divide between eating and cooking areas. Special installation is required for both tiles and glass.

Metal

Of all materials, stainless steel provides the ultimate surface: it is heatproof, non-corrosive, hygienic, shock-absorbing, and easily cleaned. Although expensive, it should last indefinitely. Other metals, including brass, chrome, aluminum, galvanized steel, and cast iron, require special care since acidic juice, cleaning chemicals, and prolonged contact with water can damage the surface.

Natural stone

Granite, slate, marble, and terra-cotta are primarily used for flooring, wall finishes, and countertops. Their beauty does not deteriorate with age and, with care, terra-cotta develops a rich patina. Natural stone is not a low-cost option, but if you plan carefully, small areas such as around the cooktop, an island, or a pastry

6

zone will look most attractive. The great weight of most natural stone and difficulty of cutting it necessitates a sturdy subframe and professional installation. Some stone, such as limestone, marble, and slate, is porous and must be sealed before use with a solvent-based sealant.

Solid surfacing, used for sinks and countertops, is made from powdered minerals bonded with acrylic and/or polyester rosins; colors and patterns can be joined seamlessly.

cross refer to
design your kitchen 34
changing cabinets 100
changing walls 102

6 Wood veneers give a more uniform finish to cabinetry. As they are usually bonded to a tough substrate such as MDF, they will not warp, shrink, or split as some solid wood finishes can.

7 Natural and artificial lighting affects various surfaces differently. The more textured a surface is, the smoother, darker, and shinier it appears. Pale surfaces create an impression of airiness.

DESIGN POINTS

■■ Prolong the life of your countertops by using chopping blocks for cutting and slicing bread, vegetables, and meat.
In a family kitchen, install cabinets that can withstand being slammed shut, knocks and bumps from toys, and regular wipe-overs.
■■ Pale surfaces lend a light, spacious feel to the kitchen but must be kept clean to maintain a pristine appearance.
■■ Avoid heavily textured surfaces for food preparation and cooking areas as dirt and grease will accumulate in crevices, making them dull and grimy.
Allow a wider gap between the counter and backsplash if using natural stone and handmade tiles as they are thicker than other finishes.
■■ Follow the manufacturers guidelines for treating wood surfaces as water, juice, and oil will seep and cause stains.

5

7

Wall surfaces

Heat, steam, and cooking residues can put unanticipated demands on kitchen wall coverings so they must be durable and washable. Pay close attention to the backsplash, around the cooktop, sink, and food preparation zone as they are subject to most wear.

1 Natural brick offers geometric pattern and texture. For protection, paint lower walls with a water-repellent sealant.

2 Stainless steel is a near-perfect surface; use a brushed finish to limit glare from reflected light.

As well as being hardwearing and stylish, you may want the wall finish to add color and interest to the kitchen. Use the color and texture of the cabinets and the type of flooring to help you find a finish that suits your overall look. Contrasting finishes work best and create a natural division between countertops and wall cabinets. Do not forget to include the cost of fitting if you opt for a finish that requires expert installation.

Suitable materials

Rough plaster and plain brick give a no-fuss, back-to-basics look to walls, adding character, although they may be porous and attract dust.

Paint is cheap and versatile. Colors can be mixed to an exact shade and paint effects can be used. Gloss and oil-based finishes repel grease and splashes but do not have the modern look of powdery matte finishes.

Vinyl wall coverings resist harsh cleaning, grease, and moisture. The paper backing helps insulate reducing condensation. Vinyl disguises uneven walls but does not suit the areas behind the oven, cooktop, and sink. Avoid cheaper, porous papers.

Ceramic tiles are durable, heat-resistant, waterproof, and washable, although grout between tiles can harbor dirt. The range of patterns, sizes, and colors available is huge.

Stainless-steel and stone such as slate and granite are durable, washable, and hygienic, but they are expensive. Limit their use, or yours may resemble a commercial kitchen.

Wood-paneling is rustic and conceals uneven walls, and can be painted or stained any color you wish.

3 Mosaic tiles are supplied on a backing sheet that is simple to cut to fit. Individual sections or tiles can be removed and swapped to form patterns.

4 Paint transforms walls quickly and changes the character and atmosphere of a room, even on a budget. Use specially formulated kitchen paint that resists staining and mildew.

5 Glass backsplashes allow the wall color to show through. They are resistant to moisture and heat, and clean easily.

cross refer to
lighting 88
cabinet finishes 94
changing walls 102

DESIGN POINTS

■■ Surround an assortment of antique tiles with a plain border to create a interesting wall panel. Place the tiles behind the range or cooktop where it will double up as a backsplash and a strong focal point.

■■ Ceramic profile strips neatly finish the edge of a run of plain tiles. They also give a tidy outline to window frames and any other recesses.

■■ Wood moldings are available in 6ft (2m) lengths and widths ranging from ½–4in (1–10cm). Use wood moldings to make a natural break between two different paint colors or wallcoverings, or to finish off tongue-and-groove paneling on lower walls.

■■ Choose a waterproof grouting material to set the tiles as this resists splashes and grease. It is easier to keep clean, and will last longer than standard cement mixes.

■■ If laminated surfaces are intended to match the cabinetry, make sure that the match is a good one as even slight differences in the surface color and finish can look obvious and ugly.

5

6

7

6 Handmade tiles, generally thicker and more expensive than manufactured ceramic tiles, add style to rooms.

7 When used over large expanses of wall, manufactured ceramic tiles offer uniformity. Coordinated ranges take the guesswork out of designing a pattern.

8 Laminated surfaces in woodgrain effects work well with plain wall colors or some textured finishes.

9 This dark granite backsplash gives the cabinets good definition.

8

9

Lighting

Kitchen lighting should be designed so that it provides a practical and pleasant environment for cooking and eating. The key to successful lighting lies in supplying a combination of task lights for working and ambient light for eating and relaxing.

Lighting must be planned and installed before cabinets, flooring, or appliances are installed. The top priority is to locate the lights strategically throughout the kitchen, bearing in mind that cooking involves constant moving between sink, refrigerator, food preparation area, and cooktop. Light should illuminate all areas adequately, including the corners: wherever you stand you should not cast a shadow over your work. Good lighting highlights potential dangers such as spills or objects on the floor, improving safety in this busy room.

Task lighting

The simplest, if least inspiring, task light is a fluorescent tube that provides a clear, bright light. These can, however, cause glare and eyestrain, so are best suited for undercabinet lighting where they cast a good light over the counter.

Pendant lights provide excellent task lighting and can improve the look of islands and peninsulas that double as eating areas. Freestanding task lights such as desk lamps and clip spotlights can be moved from one position to another as needed. Provide sufficient electrical outlets so cords do not trail across the floor.

Ceiling downlights can be fixed spotlights or multidirectional eyeball lights. Recessed at regular intervals in the ceiling, they give out a strong, directional light and as they lie flush, dirt and dust will not settle on them.

Track lights to suit all tastes are available, from hi-tech chrome and halogen arcs to those with country-

style wood fittings. The principal advantage of track systems is that one outlet operates up to six lights, reducing the cost of installation. The lamps are multidirectional, so they can be focused onto different areas.

Atmospheric lighting

Wall lights fit flush to the wall and cast light onto the ceiling, creating a soft light for dining. Freestanding uplights that cast glare-free illumination above eye-level achieve the same effect – use them in larger kitchens as they need floor space. Pendant and multi-arm lights focus on eating areas and look best when other kitchen lighting is switched off. Rise-and-fall light shades can be raised to allow more headroom if necessary. Candlelight is the most evocative, perfect for special meals.

1 Fluorescent strips or low-voltage halogen lamps called puck lights can be cleverly hidden underneath wall cabinets. They cast light directly over food preparation areas.

2 A series of recessed downlights combined with undercabinet lighting and the illuminated cooktop ensures that there is good ambient light.

3 Natural light floods into the kitchen through full-height glass doors, pulling the garden into the kitchen and increasing the feel of light and spaciousness.

4 Lighting combined with the ventilation hood focuses light over the cooktop. Installation is simpler and cheaper than in separate units.

DESIGN POINTS

◪ Fluorescent and low-energy bulbs offer bright, shadowless light, and use less electricity. They remain cool, which makes them practical for kitchens that become very hot during use.

◪ Fluorescent tubes shed a harsh, glaring light which can cause eyestrain, so they are best shielded. Low-energy bulbs with a shade are another option.

▦ Make sure that any pendant fixtures are positioned well away from heat sources such as cooktops and ovens.

◪ Fit undercabinet lights behind the trim along the base of the wall cabinet to act as a shield, protecting your eyes from glare, but not reducing the light cast on the countertop.

▥ Wall shades made from plaster can be painted to match the decor.

▦ If the kitchen ceiling is cast from a solid material such as concrete, a false ceiling will need to be fitted to allow downlights to be recessed.

◪ Halogen lamps become extremely hot, producing a bright white light that is literally white hot. Make sure that they are kept out of reach of children.

cross refer to
design your kitchen 34 ☑
activity areas 54 ☑
serving & eating 66 ☑
quick-fix changes 98 ☑

5 Halogen track lighting can create visual interest over large expanses of wall or ceiling. Halogen bulbs last longer than tungsten bulbs but are fragile: handle with care when replacing them.

6 Candelabras cast soft, flattering light over the table; providing the perfect finishing touch when entertaining.

7 Freestanding lights can illuminate the eating area when strong task lights are switched off.

8 A contemporary rise-and-fall pendant light is lowered for dining.

4

5

6

7

8

Flooring

Floorings suited to the heavy wear in kitchens include natural stone, wood, ceramic

tile, vinyl, laminates, and linoleum. They all offer durability and ease of maintenance –

but consider also factors such as budget, comfort, and surrounding surfaces.

1 Once properly sealed, limestone tiles resist water, heat, and household chemicals.

2 Rubber stud flooring is expensive but easy to install and so tough that it is regularly used for public buildings.

The floor is the most visible area of the kitchen and can alter the look of the whole room. If it links living and dining areas, consider using one flooring, as contrasting colors or patterns may conflict. Floorings can affect noise levels, so check if your choice has sound-deadening properties to muffle footsteps or whether it will exacerbate them. Look at the safety aspect to assess whether the flooring is slip-resistant when wet and whether splashes are easy to see before they cause an accident.

Material advantages

Wood is resilient, warm underfoot, and available in a range of colors and patterns. Tile and stone are resistant to water, heat, and chemicals but are noisy, cold, and hard on the feet. Laminates have a moisture-resistant backing and are hardwearing; they are available in a variety of effects and colors. Vinyl is durable, warm, and quiet underfoot, with many style options. Linoleum is hardwearing and easy to clean, and is made from natural materials, such as linseed.

2

3

3 Textured metal stud floors add great style to contemporary kitchens. This material is durable, easy to clean, and reflects light. The drawbacks are that it is expensive, noisy, and requires quite a high level of maintenance.

cross refer to
design your kitchen 34
activity areas 54
kitchen materials 84
cabinet finishes 94

6 Wood floorings are reasonably priced and warm underfoot, but they can be damaged by heavy furniture and must be well maintained to avoid moisture penetration. The color and grain add character and warmth to kitchens.

7 Slate is popular for its cool, clean look, which blends with any cabinet style. It is hard and cold underfoot, but will last a lifetime.

4 Terra-cotta flooring has a naturally warm look that develops a rich patina over time. It is hardwearing and comfortable to walk on without shoes.

5 Glazed ceramic tiles should have a matte finish or be textured to make them anti-slip. Rough surfaces that incorporate a fine grit in the glaze are practical in busy kitchens. Ceramic tiles are extremely durable, water- and heat-resistant, and easy to wipe clean.

DESIGN POINTS

The flooring you choose must be laid on a good subfloor or it will wear unevenly and the manufacturer's warranty will be invalidated.

Test sheet vinyl for impact resistance by pressing the edge of a coin hard into the surface to see if it leaves an indentation or recovers quickly.

Choose flooring tiles that are in proportion to the size of the room. For example, use large format tiles for big kitchens and small ones for studios and one-wall galleys.

Avoid placing mats or rugs over pale flooring as daylight and everyday wear will gradually change the patina on both natural and man-made products.

Remember that terra-cotta and other porous stone floorings require sealing before use or they may stain if they come into contact with grease.

7

Countertops

Countertops play a vital role in the smooth running of kitchen activities. As well as enhancing kitchen style, they must be be durable and resistant to heat, stains, sharp knives, moisture, and abrasive cleaning, so consider the properties of each type.

There is no single, multipurpose surface to cope with the demands of all kitchen activities. Look at the properties each surface offers and plan to include at least two different types in your kitchen. The surface most suited to chopping and slicing is endgrain wood, which will not be damaged by sharp blades. For pastry rolling choose marble and, in cooking areas, stone or tiles are best for resisting hot pans. A chopping block or marble slab recessed into the countertop is ideal for food preparation areas and is always ready for use. Alternatively, keep a range of chopping boards close to where they will be needed.

Points to consider

Stainless steel gives the best all-round performance as it is heatproof, hygienic, and hardwearing. Granite will not stain, chip or scratch and is heat- and waterproof. It stays cool and is a perfect surface for rolling pastry and preparing meat and fish. Both stainless steel and granite are expensive and require professional installation. Wood is ideal for food preparation, but must be treated to prevent moisture from causing warping and the joins to open.

Laminated counters are popular as they are affordable and available in many colors and designs. The surface resists stains, abrasive cleaning, and moisture, but sharp knives and heat can damage it. Solid surfacing is a versatile material made from a blend of mineral powders and rosins. If damaged, the surface can simply be sanded down to remove the marks.

1 High-gloss surfaces add an interesting perspective to counters as they reflect images and light for an ever-changing look.

2 The natural grain and warm coloring of lacquered wood countertops complement most kitchen cabinetry.

3 Stone surfaces are cool to the touch and resist heat. Granite is the most durable and comes in a wide range of colors.

4 Corian® is made from mineral powders and resins; the color is solid throughout so it does not require an edge trim to conceal the substrate.

5 Stone counters can be routed to help with drainage, eliminating the need for a combined sink/draining board.

6 The deep color of this lacquered wood counter complements the pale tone of the cabinetry.

7 Stainless-steel counters are ideal in the sink and stovetop areas as they are water- and heat-resistant.

8 Match countertops to the function for which they will be used. Here, heat- and water-resistant counters are used in the cooking/sink zones and wood in the food preparation island.

3

4

5

DESIGN POINTS

As a guide, the most expensive option is stone, followed by solid surfacing, tile, wood, and then laminate. Simple, straight runs of counter are the least expensive to install. Add extra for layouts that include bake centers, additional sinks, and islands.

Choose counters with rounded, postformed, or bullnose edges to eliminate sharp corners that could hurt if knocked against.

Tiled counters work well around the cooking area because they are heat-resistant, but grout can collect dirt and may be difficult to clean.

Try to include two height levels so that activities, such as baking are comfortable and convenient.

Plan the backsplash area at the same time as the countertop so that the two complement each other.

6

cross refer to
activity areas 54
chopping & rinsing 60
mixing 60
sinks & faucets 78

7

8

Cabinet finishes

The character of your kitchen will be influenced by the cabinet finish, but give priority to practical considerations. Surfaces that receive intensive use and are subjected to daily heat and moisture require a finish that does not rely on good looks alone.

Start by considering who will use the kitchen and how often, then find out as much as possible about the different finishes. How easy it is to maintain? Does it absorb or reflect light? Can it be damaged by cleaning fluids? Will knocks dent or chip the surface? Once you have eliminated those finishes unlikely to stand the test of time, you can then concentrate on choosing the color and design you want.

Natural materials

Wood, either solid or veneered, is the most widely used finish for cabinets. Contrary to popular belief, veneers are often preferable to solid woods as the base to which they are bonded will not warp, shrink, or split with changing temperatures and humidity. Hardwood veneers are often applied over MDF (medium density fiberboard), but cheaper softwood veneers may be bonded to particleboard, which is prone to denting and can swell or "blow" if moisture penetrates the finish. The beauty of veneers is that they provide uniform graining and, as such thin sections can be cut, a small amount of wood goes a long way.

Metals & laminates

Aluminum, galvanized finishes, and stainless steel all have designer status, but the latter is most suited to kitchens, with its non-corrosive, heat- and waterproof qualities. Polyester coatings give a high-gloss finish that resists steam and is easily cleaned; they are generally applied over MDF, which is strong and can be routed to

achieve molded detail. High-pressure laminates consist of layers of rosin and paper compressed under heat. They are more expensive and more durable than low-pressure laminates, but both come in assorted textures, patterns, and colors. Thermafoil finishes consist of a plastic sheet that bonds to a base material when heated. It molds to the shape of the substrate and is more durable than lacquered, low-pressure laminates and some polyester finishes. Their big advantage is that painted finishes closely resemble hand-crafted designs but cost significantly less.

1

2

3

1 Polyester finishes are sophisticated and hardwearing, but are more expensive than laminates and lacquers. They are easily cleaned, though abrasive cloths and cleaners will dull the finish.

2 Laminated cabinets here are framed with natural wood to add interest, and complemented by opaque glass-fronted cabinets and open shelving to provide display areas.

3 Bright metal trims and drawer knobs turn a functional cabinet into an eye-catching feature. The ridged sides of the cabinets and opaque glass drawer fronts add to the overall effect.

4 Stainless-steel cabinets can seem utilitarian if used throughout the kitchen. A good balance has been achieved here by blending them with wood base cabinets fitted with long stainless-steel handles.

5 Lacquered finishes are spray-painted onto a colored base to provide a tough, protective finish. They are a good alternative to expensive polyester finishes.

6 When using wood finishes over large areas, look out for consistency of grain and color as differences will be obvious.

DESIGN POINTS

Look at showroom cabinets and inspect areas that receive the heaviest wear, such as around the edges, hinges, and seams, to spot any possible signs of weakness in the materials.

Glass-fronted cabinets allow items stored inside to be located before the door is opened. They also help to create a light and spacious atmosphere in small kitchens.

Choose a combination of cabinet finishes, such as a laminate panel with natural wood, to prevent large expanses of color or texture from becoming overpowering or monotonous.

4

5

cross refer to

wall cabinets 36

base cabinets 38

food storage areas 56

changing cabinets 100

7 Factory paint finishes are sprayed in large batches for a smooth, uniform surface. Colors can be matched to your scheme and coordinating shades chosen for trims and moldings.

6

7

Traditional finishes

The one material that looks as good in modern settings as it does in traditional rooms is wood. It is supremely versatile and the infinite variety of color and grain make sure that no two kitchens are alike.

Whether traditional, highly carved oak, contemporary maple, or timeless Shaker cherry, kitchens using wood have instant appeal, character, and style. But the true beauty of wood is that, as it ages, the effects of wear, polishing, and daylight produce a rich patina. Wooden surfaces are a pleasure to touch: it is difficult to resist running your hand over a simple tabletop or molding when the shape, grain, and finish have been beautifully crafted.

Wood types

Hardwoods, including ash, beech, cherrywood, London plane, oak, and maple, are more expensive than softwoods as the trees take many years to reach a usable size. They have a dense, heavy grain, and are less likely to split, dent, warp, and rot than softwoods. Pine is the most commonly used softwood and includes redwood or Scotch pine,

Parana, ponderosa, pitch, yellow, and white pine. Spruce, larch, and fir are also used for kitchen cabinets.

Both hardwood and softwood can be stained, limed, distressed, or finished with paint effects. Veneers make careful use of exotic woods by slicing them into thin "leaves" that are bonded to a material such as MDF. Burr woods and interesting graining are left in their natural state so the color and detail become the focal point of the cabinet design.

DESIGN POINTS

■■ To get the best results and to make sure that solid wood cabinets are well maintained, polish the fronts in the direction of the wood grain and buff regularly with a soft cloth.

■■ Wood moldings and simple trims add character to plain cabinet fronts. Rounded door knobs and carved wood panels give cabinetry classic style.

■■ Natural stone floor tiles and plain whitewashed walls help emphasize the beauty of natural wood finishes.

■■ Veneered finishes are not suitable for areas where they are likely to get a regular drenching from water.

1 A traditional dresser combines the natural beauty of wood with classic craftsmanship skills. The rounded legs together with the simple carved detailing make this piece the focal point of the kitchen room.

cross refer to
wall cabinets 36
base cabinets 38
sinks & faucets 78
kitchen materials 84

2 Distressed finishes transform new wood to give it the patina of a year's worth of care and wear. The panels and small door handles add cottage-style charm.

3 Limed finishes give wood a pale, grainy look that is lighter and more adaptable than heavily colored stains.

4 The deep colors of these hand-painted wooden cabinets are offset by the white ceramic sink, pale walls, and the textural qualities of a wicker laundry basket.

QUICK FIXES

Quick-fix changes

If your kitchen already has a perfectly functional layout but looks slightly lackluster, there are new ideas and designs that you can utilize to improve its appearance without going to the expense of a complete refit.

1 Brighten up your kitchen with a set of colorful chairs. If space is tight, choose a stackable design so they can be put to one side after meals and to make room when cleaning.

When a kitchen is used everyday, it is easy to overlook slight irritations and inefficient equipment when you are concentrating on the main tasks such as preparing meals and cleaning up afterward. But take a few moments to make a note of the areas that could be updated or changed to make working in the kitchen on a daily basis more of a pleasure.

Ask yourself about the amount of clutter that stays out on the countertops and how easy it is clean around them. Would you like to replace the counters to include different materials to suit pastry-making, for example, or include a wooden chopping surface? Look at the internal fittings of drawers: do they make it easy to find utensils?

2 A wedge-shaped tabletop utilizes a small space at the end of a run of cabinets to create a dining area. Lightweight chairs maintain the feeling of space.

Think about meal times: does the furniture interrupt the smooth flow of activities? Is it comfortable and practical for every family member? Once you have considered every aspect, you will be able to prioritize and gradually introduce changes to kitchen fittings that will improve your everyday working environment.

Furniture & fittings

If there is insufficient space in your kitchen to sit and eat snacks, and you find yourself perching against a counter to save time, consider the possibilities of a small eating area at the end of a run of cabinets. A drop-down table or custom-made tabletop to fit the available space will help make breakfasts more relaxing

and pleasurable. Where existing furniture takes up valuable floor space, look at alternative furniture such as drop-leaf tables and folding or stacking chairs to allow greater freedom of movement. Scrutinize your storage facilities to assess whether your existing arrangements work efficiently and if space exists that could be used to house cooking items cluttering surfaces.

Light & color

Just as well-planned lighting can improve working conditions, so can improved natural daylight. Over-fussy window treatments and shades can block out light and make a room seem gloomy and dull. Look at the possibilities of changing the fabric

3 A custom-made plate draining rack is situated near to the sink and fully utilizes the alcove next to the chimney breast. Shelves above the sink are used to store stacks of plates, and mugs hang from hooks along the edges.

2

3

cross refer to
storing kitchenware 58
serving & eating 66
kitchen materials 84
lighting 88

DESIGN POINTS

Choose furnishings that are easily removed for cleaning, and fittings that can be wiped over to remove dust.

A hanging rack over an island is useful for keeping food preparation equipment within reach.

If the counter is used as secondary storage, find an attractive basket or box to keep oils, seasonings, spices, and fresh herbs neatly together and where they can be moved in one easy step to clean underneath.

Clear kitchen counters by removing clutter and seldom-used gadgets into nearby cabinets. If necessary, buy a selection of baskets and sweep odds and ends into one container to hold all the pens and pencils, that have no specific place of their own.

4 Replace furnishings with light fabrics in bright colors to update the kitchen. Keep the window treatments simple to allow the maximum penetration of natural light.

5 A slatted storage system is inexpensive, versatile and space-saving. Butchers' hooks can be moved to any level so that utensils and pans are kept within easy reach.

6 Inexpensive shelving, with slatted doors below, turn this alcove into an attractive dresser for displaying plates.

5

and fittings to give the kitchen a bright, fresh look. Use coordinating fabrics and colors for seat covers and table linens so that the style is echoed throughout the room.

Flooring

Worn flooring can not only ruin the effect of other items in the room, it can be dangerous too. Where there are solid wood floorboards, consider sanding them down to remove the surface varnish, and color-washing or stenciling a border or overall design across the surface. Once dry, the wood can be sealed with two or three coats of clear polyurethane varnish to protect the pattern from wear and cleaning.

Solid stone flooring can lose its luster and joins can become grimy after a while. It is possible, but quite hard work to sand the surface to bring back the original color. If you do think it is worthwhile, try a small patch in an inconspicuous area first. Once cleaned, make sure that the joins are renewed and then check that the flooring is properly sealed before use.

4

6

Changing cabinets

General wear and tear and changing fashions can soon make kitchen cabinets look tired and in need of a facelift. If the internal fittings and space allocation are satisfactory, aim to transform the exterior with the minimum of effort and expense.

There are several ways to modernize and improve cabinets. Some require more effort than others, but all will alter the kitchen's character and extend the life of the cabinets. New cabinet doors are a simple but expensive option; adding moldings or fabric panels and changing the handles and knobs gives new visual interest; but the quickest and least expensive way of transforming kitchen cabinets is to repaint them.

Cabinet facelift

Whether your existing kitchen was fitted with a custom-made or stock foundation, the units behind the doors will be relatively similar. Plywood, hardwood, MDF, and particleboard are widely used to make drawers and frames. If they are sound, it is perfectly feasible to simply change the face of them by replacing the door and drawer fronts. Whether you choose wood for a country style or the city chic of high-gloss polyester finishes, there are certain companies which will supply new cabinet fronts for you and a carpenter to install them.

Wood moldings are available in a variety of designs. They are ideal for creating panels on flat laminate doors and drawers. Wider moldings can be used as cornicing along the top of wall cabinets, or fitted as a decorative means to conceal under-cabinet lighting. Stain or paint them to match existing cabinets.

Decorative touches

Stenciling, marbling, dragging, and other popular paint effects require a little practice to get the technique

right but, once mastered, they offer infinite variety. If you would like a dramatic and modern effect, pierce a design on metal and secure the panel to the existing cabinet front.

For a simple change, replace the hardware and hinges with surface-mounted fittings to create a bold, contemporary look. Gun-metal or wrought-iron hinges and fittings are ideal for Gothic-style kitchen cabinets, or choose unusual ceramic and clear acrylic designs for plain-colored cabinets.

1 Give reproduction pine dressers a new lease of life with boldly colored paint and contrasting door and drawer knobs.

2 Well-worn but good quality cupboard interiors look interesting and modern when painted in a neutral color. Use enamel spray paints, which are easy to apply, quick-drying, and incredibly hardwearing.

3 Pewter paint kits and metallic spray paints give a dramatic finish to cabinet fronts. Complete the makeover by replacing old door and drawer knobs with new, more decorative fittings.

1

2

6

cross refer to

wall cabinets 36

base cabinets 38

kitchen materials 84

cabinet finishes 94

DESIGN POINTS

When replacing doors, it is important to check that existing hinges can be reused or are easily replaced, as the cabinet sides may be damaged or weakened by screw holes and recesses where the original hinges were fitted.

■■ Different finishes affect the quality of light in kitchens, so remember that shiny finishes reflect light but can cause glare, whereas matte finishes absorb and diffuse light and give a softer look.

■■ If choosing fabric door infills, make sure that the fabric is machine-washable.

■■ When painting cabinet fronts, it is best to remove them by unscrewing their hinges. Place them on a flat surface so that the paint does not drip.

■■ Always provide a good base for paint and glue to adhere properly by cleaning and sanding the cabinet door surface before applying a coat of paint.

4

5

4 Fabric cabinet fronts have a softer, country look and are ideal if you want to create a Shaker-style kitchen. When the fabric needs washing, simply remove it from the net wires that hold it securely in place.

5 Stainless-steel or aluminum panels can be fitted over existing cabinetry with the minimum of cost and disruption. Replace hardware and small appliances at the same time for a well-coordinated look.

7

6 Use the panel on the dishwasher that matches the cabinets as a template for the new finish. If painting, remove the panel and paint or spray it away from the appliance.

7 Chunky hardware instantly updates cabinets. Make sure the style you choose is available in at least two sizes so that large cabinets or small drawers maintain a balanced look.

8 Depending on your preferences, cut-out detailing and finger-hole pulls can be designed in contemporary geometric or traditional floral patterns. Once the template has been made, it can be used as a stencil guide to create a visual link between the kitchen cabinetry and wall finish.

9 Punched metal infills are best fitted to flat panels. The rough edge can be sharp, so make sure that it is concealed or covered by a trim.

8

9

Changing wall finishes

Tiles, paint, natural stone, wallpapers, and wood give visual impact to kitchen walls and backsplashes. An infinite variety of effects can be achieved by combining different colors and textures to create a distinctive look that not only enhances your existing kitchen cabinetry, but links together the different elements that make up your kitchen.

Wall surfaces usually comprise a series of blocks separated by cabinets, appliances, doors, and windows. Aim for a common link by selecting a design or color to complement the cabinetry, flooring, and counters. Make sure that kitchen wall surfaces can resist steam, moisture, and occasional cleaning.

New looks

A coat of paint is the easiest and least expensive fix for kitchen walls. For interest, stencil a border or cover them with a stamped pattern. Use metallic paints to catch the light and to enhance other metallic finishes in the room. Consider fitting tongue-and-grooved paneling for a country-cottage style, or covering walls with a rough plaster finish to conjure up the image of Mediterranean interiors. Once painted, the effect adds interest without becoming too busy.

The backsplash is an ideal area to introduce pattern and color. Tiles are very hardwearing, and the layout of hand-painted designs, relief tiles, and solid colors could echo shades used elsewhere in the room.

Vinyl wallcoverings are quick and inexpensive to put up, and many form part of coordinated schemes that include borders, shades, and fabrics. For the best effect, choose plain-colored towels and table linen to accent one of the colors in the wallcovering design.

1 A row of brightly colored handmade tiles add visual interest to the backsplash area behind the kitchen sink and are inexpensive to buy in small quantities. Individual tiles can be selected to accent your choice of linens.

1

DESIGN POINTS

■■ It is always best to remove old wallcoverings before hanging a new one as grease and imperfections can work their way through the layers.

■■ Use several tile colors as accents in the backsplash, and emphasize one with matching linens. When it's time for a change, replace the window treatments, towels, and wall color with a different shade from the backsplash.

■■ Whitewash the walls to add a crisp, fresh look to kitchens. It adapts as well to battered antique finishes as it does to gleaming stainless steel.

■■ Shades of blue, green, and gray are cool colors but can appear harsh on wintry days. Shades of yellow, orange, and pink are warm and create a cozy, homey kitchen atmosphere.

2 Replace wallcoverings regularly to keep the room looking clean and fresh. To divide large expanses of wall, choose wallcoverings that coordinate. A textural effect beneath the border and a striped design above helps to reduce the impact of a high ceiling.

2

cross refer to
sinks & faucets 78
kitchen materials 84
wall surfaces 86
cabinet finishes 94

5 Tongue-and-grooved paneling is easy to install. It can be stained and painted in any color, it is hardwearing, and acts as an insulator. For a neater finish, trim the top edge with a decorative molding or wood strip.

6 A multicolored backsplash brings color to a plain kitchen. Choose kitchen linens to accent one color; when they become worn, select another for a completely fresh look.

5

3

3 To give the room contemporary style, paint one wall in a bold color to echo the hues of the window treatment and linens.

4 The backsplash behind the cooktop or range should withstand heat, steam, grease, and splashes. Paint is the least expensive option, but choose an oil-based paint such as eggshell or gloss that dries to a hardwearing finish.

4

6

Adding details

An interesting collection of utensils, tableware, or a rack of gleaming kitchen accessories create

essential focal points around the room. Unless collectables can be easily wiped clean of

kitchen dust and grease, place them in glass-fronted cabinets that are quick to wash down.

1 Attractive, well-designed accessories, such as this corkscrew and pepper mill, are perfectly suited for kitchen display.

2 A deep backsplash doubles as a shelf for displaying utensils. Butchers' hooks are suspended from the overhead rail to display miscellaneous practical kitchen accessories where they are easy to find.

3 This wallmounted rack offers a shelf for a jumble of interesting pans, and assorted kitchenware is suspended underneath from butchers' hooks.

Whether you thrive in a kitchen surrounded by collectables, or cannot function unless every surface is clear, redecorating is a good time to organize kitchen accessories into manageable groups and interesting displays. Consider how you want your kitchen to look and function: do you want it to be contemporary and sleek, or traditional and homey? Once you have decided, select the items that you feel most enhance the style, and plan where they can be displayed appropriately.

Contemporary look

The products that look best in contemporary kitchens have a bold, simple shape and minimal pattern. Texture and color are key factors for adding interest. Materials are functional and include stainless steel, frosted glass, and natural wood. The best colors are bright – kitchen accessories and tableware in zingy citrus colors add style and interest. Stainless-steel utensils and pans maintain a good finish so are ideal for leaving on display. Open-grid shelving adds contemporary style but looks good only if your selection of fruit and vegetables stored inside are crisp and fresh.

High-tech kettles, toasters, food mixers, or salt and pepper mills that remain on the kitchen countertop will make a practical design statement. Finishes in chrome or stainless steel reflect light and look efficient, but anything that is less than pristine should be stored where it will not detract from the overall effect you are trying to create.

Traditional look

Traditional kitchens include elements that have been collected, or handed down from one generation to the next, over the years. Colors are mixed with checks and floral patterns to add an informal touch. Aim to mix functional items with decorative accessories. Modern gadgetry will distract from the overall look so store them in an appliance garage where they are ready for use but out of sight. Providing everything is clean, wood surfaces with a well-worn patina and the odd paint imperfection create a relaxed and uncontrived look.

cross refer to
choosing a style 16
wall cabinets 36
storing kitchenware 58
wall surfaces 86

4 For efficient and space-saving kitchen storage, look for surface-mounted stainless-steel systems that can be put together in any combination to suit the available space.

5 An inexpensive punched aluminum wall rack offers neat and unobtrusive storage for small accessories.

6 Hanging racks make full use of the ceiling space above counters, and create a display of attractive pans and kitchen utensils.

7 A series of wardrobe support bars make excellent racks for kitchen paraphernalia. Available from most good hardware stores in white, chrome, brass, and nickel they will blend easily with most cabinet finishes.

8 Making a feature of colorful fruit and vegetables – a cart with metal grid shelving can be moved freely around the room and allows air to circulate around the fresh contents.

9 The open shelving of this metal bottle rack allows labels to be read easily and keeps the kitchen looking spacious and airy.

10 Original Shaker paint colors are muted, but peg-rails can be just as eyecatching in bright acid colors and paint-effect finishes.

11 Wallmounted rails make full use of the space above your head, providing attractive and practical storage within arm's reach. Space between the bars allows you to view items stacked on top.

DESIGN POINTS

A display of bright white plates or sparkling glasses makes an inexpensive and functional kitchen feature.

Antique canisters or pots of well-worn utensils add character to traditional kitchens.

Mix three or four bright citrus colors together for contemporary style.

Gingham checks and delicate floral fabrics add cottage-style charm.

Display fresh or dried culinary herbs by suspending them from a rack.

Directory

The following directory of useful names and addresses will help you source all the products needed to furnish and equip your kitchen.

A brief description is given of each to help you make your choice.

Appliances

Admiral Home Appliances
740 King Edward Ave
Cleveland. TN 37311
Tel: 615-472-3371
Major kitchen appliances
see p81 (3)

Aga Cookers Inc
RFD 1, Box 477
Stowe. VT 05672
Tel: 802-253-9727
Gas, electric, and solid fuel cooking/heating ranges
see p73 (6)

Amana Home Appliances
2800 220th Trail
PO Box 8901
Amana. IA 52204
Tel: 800-843-0304
Ranges, cooktops, refrigerator/freezers, dishwashers, microwaves, and air conditioners

Antique Stove Heaven
5414 Southwestern Ave
Los Angeles. CA 90062
Tel: 213-298-5581
Antique, re-conditioned stoves

Bisque Radiators
244 Belsize Road
London. NW6 4BT
Tel: 0044-1328-2225
Colorful and contemporary radiators
see p34 (2)

Cole's Appliance & Furniture Co
4026 Lincoln Ave
Chicago. IL 60618
Tel: 773-525-1797
Appliances, electronics, home furnishings

Creda Inc
5700 West Touhy Ave
Chicago. IL 60648
Tel: 708-647-6917
Washer/dryers, refrigeration

Dacor
Distinctive Appliance Corporation
950 South Raymond Ave
Pasadena. CA 91109
Tel: 626-441-9632
Cooktops, ranges, ovens, hoods and vents, warming ovens, and cooktop modules

Fivestar
c/o Brown Stove Works, Inc
PO Box 2490
Cleveland. TN 37320
Tel: 423-476-6544
Manufacturers of ranges

Frigidaire Co
PO Box 7181
Dublin. OH 43017
Tel: 800-685-6005
Dishwashers, ranges, cooktops, fridge-freezers, microwaves, washers, and dryers

Gaggenau USA Corp
425 University Ave
Norwood. MA 02062
Tel: 617-255-1766
Cooktops, modules, steamers, ovens
see p71 (7)

GE Appliances
General Electric
AP 35- Room 1007B
Appliance Park
Louisville. KY 40225
Tel: 800-626-2000
Cooktops, fridge-freezers, microwaves, and dishwashers
see pp64 (3), 72 (4), 75 (13), 77 (4, 8), 82 (4)

Gringer & Sons
29 First Avenue
New York. NY 10003
Tel: 212-475-0600
Household appliances and mail order available

Heartland Appliances Inc
5 Hoffman Street
Kitchener
Ontario. N2M 3M5
Tel: 800-361-1517
Traditionally-styled ranges, ovens, and refrigerators
see pp73 (5), p75 (4)

Jenn-Air
240 Edwards Street SE
Cleveland. TN 37311
Tel: 800-536-6247
Appliance and ventilation system manufacturer
see pp65 (6), 75 (5)

KitchenAid
2000 M-63
Mail Drop 4302
Benton Harbor. MI 49022
Tel: 800-253-3977
Cooktops, ranges, fridge-freezers, dishwashers, microwaves, air conditioners; food garbage and trash compactors

Maytag Co
403 West 4th Street North
Newton. IA 50208
Tel: 800-688-9900
Cooktops, ranges, dishwashers, fridge-freezers, microwaves, and air conditoning units, including Magic Chef and Admiral brands

Miele Appliances
22D World's Fair Drive
Somerset. NJ 08873
Tel: 800-843-7231
Cooktops, ranges, dishwashers, vacuums, and microwaves, including Imperial steam ovens
see pp75 (6, 7, 8, 9, 10), 80 (4)

Professional Home Kitchens
1504 145th Place
SE Boulevard. WA 98007
Commercial-style Lacanche stoves, and stainless-steel refrigerators
see pp6 (1), 69, 70 (1)

Sub-zero Freezer Co Inc
PO Box 4130
Madison. WI 53744
Tel: 800-444-7820
Wide range of fridge-freezers with attractive finishes and door styles
see pp38 (2), 55 (6), 56 (3), 77 (7), 79 (7)

Tappan Appliances
6000 Perimeter Drive
Dublin. OH 43017
Tel: 800-685-6005
Wide range of major kitchen appliances

Thermador, Masco Corp
5119 District Blvd
Los Angeles. CA 90040
Tel: 213-562-1133
Cooktops, ranges, and major appliances

Viking Range Corp
111 Front Street
Greenwood. MS 38930
Tel: 601-455-1200
Professional quality ranges, ovens, ventilation systems, fridge-freezers, and food waste disposals
see pp72 (2), 73 (7), 76 (1), 77 (6), 80 (3)

Whirlpool Corp
2000 M-63
Mail Drop 4303
Benton Harbor. MI 49022
Tel: 800-253-1301
All major kitchen appliances
see p81 (1, 4)

White-Westinghouse
Frigidaire Co.
6000 Perimeter Drive
Dublin. OH 43017
Tel: 800-374-4434
All major kitchen appliances

Cabinetry

Allmilmo Corp
P.O. Box 629
70 Clinton Road
Fairfield. NJ 07004
Tel: 201-227-2502
Contemporary cabinets in most finishes

Boffi Arredamento Cucina, SPA
Via G Oberdan
20030 Lentate Sul Seveso
Milan. Italy
Contemporary fitted, and stainless steel cabinetry
see pp36 (4), 45 (5), 46 (1), 47 (5), 49 (5),
54 (1), 59 (4), 67 (6), 87 (8)

Bulthaup Corp
Los Angeles. CA
Tel: 310-288-3875 for catalog
Wood, stainless steel, and glass contemporary fitted
and freestanding kitchen designs
see pp2, 6 (2, 3), 7 (6), 16 (1), 33, 36 (3, 5),
37 (7), 38 (1), 39 (6, 7, 11), 41 (4), 46 (2), 48 (2),
51 (7), 52 (3), 53, 54 (3), 55 (4), 56 (1), 58 (3),
60 (2), 61 (3), 62 (1), 70 (2), 75 (3), 79 (6, 8),
82 (1, 5), 83, 86 (2), 87 (5), 89 (4), 94 (1)

Camargue plc
Townsend Farm Road
Houghton Regis
Bedfordshire. LU5 5BA
Tel: 0044-158269-9122
Contemporary cabinet styles and finishes
see pp17, 19, 21, 23, 25, 27, 29, 31

Chalon Ltd
c/o Guy Chaddock & Co
San Francisco Design Center
Suite 480, 101 Henry Adams Street
San Francisco. CA 94103
Tel: 415-621-8828
Freestanding, traditional custom kitchens in solid
wood and antiqued paint finishes
see pp41 (3), 65 (4), 67 (4), 82 (2), 85 (7),
88 (2), 96 (2)

Conran's Habitat
160 E. 54th Street
New York. NY 10003
Tel: 800-3-CONRAN
Freestanding kitchen cabinets, and accessories
see pp98 (1), 104 (1)

Crabtree Kitchens
Herbert House
Lower Station Approach Road
Temple Meads
Bristol. BS1 6QS
Tel: 0044-117929-2293
Custom-made kitchens in a variety of woods
see pp39 (9), 44 (1, 2), 45 (6), 49 (4), 55 (5),
56 (2), 58 (1), 64 (2), 78 (1), 85 (6), 87 (9),
88 (1)

European Country Kitchens
49 Route 202 PO Box 117
Far Hills. NJ 07931
Tel: 908-781-1554
Traditional cabinetry

Fulham Kitchens
19 Carnwath Road
Fulham
London. SW6 3HR
Tel: 0044-171736-6458
Comtemporary and traditional kitchen styles
see pp43 (4), 50 (2), 60 (1), 62 (3), 66 (2),
92 (1), 93 (6), 101 (7)

Ikea US Inc
Plymouth Commons
Plymouth Meting. PA 19462
Tel: 412-747-0747
Swedish budget flat-pack kitchens in solid wood and
laminate finishes

Keith Gray & Co
Great Priory Farm
Panfield
Braintree
Essex. CM7 5BQ
Tel: 0044-137632-8540
Makers of fine bespoke furniture
see pp16 (2), 37 (8), 39 (5), 45 (6), 50 (1),
51 (5), 54 (2), 57 (6), 78 (2), 93 (3,5), 96 (3),
100 (1)

Kraftmaid Cabinetry
P.O. Box 1055
16052 Industrial Parkway
Middlefield. OH 44062
Tel: 216-632-5333
Wide range of cabinet styles and finishes

Merillat Industries, Inc
MASCO Corp.
P.O. Box 1946
5353 West US 223
Adrian. MI 49921
Tel: 517-263-0771
Custom cabinetry in wood and laminate finishes

Newcastle Furniture Co
128 Walham Green Court
Moore Park Road
London. SW6 4DG
Tel: 0044-171371-0052
Shaker-style and solid wood custom kitchens
see pp51 (7), 99 (5)

Plain English Design Ltd
The Tannery
Combs
Stowmarket
Suffolk. IP14 2EN
Tel: 0044-144977-4028
Beautiful cabinets in natural wood and National Trust
paint colors
see pp15, 18, 20, 22, 24, 26, 28, 30, 32, 96 (4)

Plain & Simple
332 Deansgate
Manchester. M3 4LY
Tel: 0044-161839-8983
Contemporary and traditional kitchens
see pp36 (2), 37 (9), 51 (4), 65 (7), 87 (6),
93 (8), 95 (4,7), 103 (6)

Poggenpohl US Inc
145 U.S. Hwy 46 West-Suite 200
Wayne. NJ 07470
Tel: 800-987-0553
Contemporary polyester, stainless steel, and laminate
custom cabinetry
see pp16 (3), 74 (1)

Roundhouse Design
25 Chalk Farm Road
London. NW1 8AG
Tel: 0044-171428-9955
Contemporary and classic bespoke kitchens
see pp35 (4), 57 (4), 71 (4)

Rutt Custom Cabinetry
HARROW Industries, Inc.
1564 Main Street
P.O. Box 129
Goodville. PA 17528
Tel: 215-445-6751
Wide range of cabinet styles and finishes

SieMatic Corporation
Two Greenwood Square
331 Street Road
Suite 450. Bensalem. PA 19020
Tel: 215-244-6800
Contemporary custom cabinetry and appliances
see pp37 (6, 10), 38 (4), 39 (10), 57 (5), 58 (2),
67 (5), 68 (2), 89 (6), 98 (2)

Smallbone, Inc
886 Town Center Drive
Langhorne. PA 19047
Tel: 215-750-1928
Traditional English-style and hand-painted custom
cabinetry
see pp40 (1), 57 (4), 96 (1)

Timberlake Cabinet Co
3102 Shawnee Drive
P.O. Box 1990
Winchester. VA 22601
Tel: 800-388-2483
Solid wood cabinetry in range of styles

Woodstock Furniture Ltd
4 William Street
Knightsbridge
London. SW1X 9HL
Tel: 0044-171245-9989
Beautifully crafted wood kitchens
see pp39 (8), 52 (2)

Countertops & Surfaces

Avonite
5100 Goldleaf Parkway
Suite 200
Los Angeles. CA 90056
Tel: 800-4-AVONITE
Solid surfacing in wide range of colors and finishes
see pp36 (1), 45 (4)

DuPont Corian®
Chestnut Run Plaza
P.O. Box 80702
Wilmington. DE 19880
Tel: 800-426-7426
Solid surfacing in wide range of colors and finishes
see p93 (4)

Formica Corporation
10155 Reading Road
Cincinnati. OH 45241
Tel: 800-367-6422
Laminate surfacing for countertops and cabinets

Stone Surfaces
80 Willow Street
East Rutherford. NJ 07073
Tel: 201-935-8803
Stone and mineral surfaces

Transolid, Inc
Solid Surface Solutions
11515 Vanstory Drive
Huntersville. NC 28078
Tel: 704-948-1927
Solid-surfacing custom shapes and finishes

Vermont Marble Co
61 Main Street
Proctor. VT 05765
Tel: 800-451-4468
Suppliers of marble and stone surfaces

Wenczel Tile Co
200 Enterprise Ave
Trenton. NJ 08638
Tel: 609-599-4503
Counter, wall, and floor tiles

Wilsonart International
2400 Wilson Place
Temple. TX 76504
Tel: 800-433-3222
Laminate for countertops and cabinets

Flooring

American Olean Tile Co
1000 Cannon Avenue
Lansdale. PA 19446
Tel: 215-855-111
Ceramic tiles

Amtico
New York. NY
Tel: 800-268-4260
Luxury vinyl flooring with C.A.D cutting system for custom designs
see pp43 (5), 91 (5)

Armstrong World Industries, Inc
Adistra Corp.
101 Union Street
Plymouth. MI 48170
Tel: 800-704-8000
Vinyl sheet and tile flooring

All State Rubber Co
105–12, 101 Avenue
Ozone Park
New York. NY 11416
Tel: 718-526-/890
Rubber flooring in a range of colors and textures
see pp23, 25, 29, 90 (2)

Congoleum
Princeton Pike Corporate Center # 2
989 Lenox Drive
Lawrenceville. NJ 08648
Tel: 800-934-3567
Vinyl flooring and other products

Country Floors
15 East 16th Street
New York. NY 10003
Tel: 212-627-8300
Ceramic, terra-cotta, hand-painted, and custom tile designs

Kahrs Swedish Prefinished Wood Floors
Tel: 800-784-8523
Stripwood flooring in wide range of shades/grains

Mannington Wood Floors
Mannington Mills, Inc
1327 Lincoln Drive
High Pond. NC 27260
Tel: 800-252-4202
Stripwood, parquet, and vinyl floorings

Tarkett
800 Lanidex Plaza
Parsippany. NJ 07054
Tel: 800-827-5388
Vinyl and wood flooring

Sinks & Faucets

American Standard, Inc
P.O. Box 6820
One Centenial Plaza
Piscataway. NJ 08855
Tel: 800-752-6292
Sinks, faucets, and fittings in all finishes

Blanco America
1050 Taylors Lane
Unit 4
Cinnaminson. NJ 08077
Tel: 609-829-2720
Sinks, faucets in stainless steel, brass, and Silacron
see pp17, 19, 21, 23, 25, 27, 29, 31

The Chicago Faucet Co
2100 S. Nuclear Drive
Des Plaines. IL 60018
Tel: 800-323-5060
Sinks, faucets, and fittings in all finishes

Delta Faucet
Masco Corporation
55 East 111 Street
Indianapolis. IN 46280
Tel: 317-848-1812
Faucets and sink accessories

Ego Amenities
74 Montauk Highway
Red Horse Plaza
East Hampton. NY 11937
Tel: 562-329-9147
Speciality sink and faucet showroom

Eljer Plumbingware
17120 Dallas Parkway
Dallas. TX 75248
Tel: 972-407-2600
Kitchen sink and faucet products

European Country Cooking
P.O. Box 154
Oldwick. NJ 08858
Tel: 0800-833-5339
Custom and special-order sinks and faucets

Franke, Inc Kitchen Systems
212 Church Road
North Wales. PA 19454
Tel: 800-626-5771
Stainless steel and colored sinks and faucets

Grohe America Inc
241 Covington Drive
Bloomingdale. IL 60108
Tel: 630-582-7711
Contemporary faucets, sinks, and accessories in stainless steel, metallic, and colored finishes

In-Sink-Erator
Emerson Electric Co.
4700 21st Street
Racine. WI 53406
Tel: 414-5540-5432
Waste disposers and trash compactors

Kohler Co
444 Highland Drive
Kohler. WI 53044
Tel: 800-456-4537
Contemporary and traditional faucets, cast iron, acrylic, stainless steel, and decorative fireclay sinks
see p84 (1)

Moen, Inc
Master Brand Industries, Inc
25300 Al Moen Drive
North Olmstead. OH 44070
Tel: 800-553-6636
Wide range of sink and faucet products — call for catalog and referral to local supplier

Window Treatments & Wallcoverings

American Blind & Wallpaper Factory
909 North Sheldon Road
Plymouth. MI 48170
Tel: 800-735-5300
Design consultancy and mail order

American Discount Wall & Window Coverings
1411 Fifth Ave
Pittsburgh. PA 15219
Tel: 800-777-2737
Custom and decorator fabrics, and mail order service

Designers Guild
Osborne & Little
90 Commerce Road
Stamford. CN 06902
Tel: 203-359-1500
Contemporary bold and traditional English fabrics and
furnishings
see pp99 (4), 102 (2), 103 (3)

Fabracadabrics
27 Leigh Street
Clinton. NJ 08809
Tel: 908-735-4757
Made-to-order furnishings

Hancock's
3841 Hinkleville Road
Paducah. KY 42001
Tel: 800-845-8723
Catalog of designer/decorator fabrics available by
mail order

Luxaflex
Hunter Douglas
2 Park Way
Route 17 South
Upper Saddle River. NJ 07458
Tel: 201-327-8200
Custom Venetian, vertical, and roller blinds – call for
nearest stockist referral

National Blind & Wallpaper Factory
400 Galleria # 400
Southfield. MI 48034
Tel: 800-477-8000
Window treatments, wall coverings, and phone/mail
order service

Lighting

Artemide Lighting
1980 New Highway
Farmingdale. NY 11735
Tel: 516-694-9292
Contemporary lighting systems

B.A. Robinson
1136 Sargent Avenue
Winnepeg. MB
Tel: 204-786-4400
Bathroom and kitchen lighting

Cooper Lighting
P.O. Box 4446
Houston. TX 77210
Tel: 713-739-5400
Lighting systems in wide range of styles

Elkay Manufacturing Company
2222 Camden Court
Oak Brook. IL 60521
Tel: 630-574-8484
Specialized and general kitchen lighting

George Kovaks Lighting Inc.
67–25 Otto Road
Glendale. NY 11385
Tel: 718-392-8190
Specialized and general kitchen lighting

Golden Valley Lighting
274 Eastchester Drive
High Point. NC 27262
Tel: 800-735-3377
Specialized and general kitchen lighting

Halo Lighting
6 W. 20th Street
New York. NY 10011
Tel: 212-645-4580
Specialized and general kitchen lighting

John Cullen Lighting
216 Fulham Road
London. SW6 9NT
Tel: 0044-171371-9000
Specializes in low-voltage kitchen lights
See pp88 (3), 89 (5)

Lightolier Inc.
100 Lighting Way
Secaucus. NJ 07096
Tel: 201-864-3000
Specialized and general kitchen lighting

Task Lighting Corporation
P.O. Box 1090
910 East 25th Street
Kearney. NE 68848
Tel: 800-445-6404
Design and manufacture of specialized
lighting systems

Hardware

Baldwin Hardware Corp
841 East Wyomissing Boulevard
P.O. Box 15048
Reading. PA 19612
Tel: 215-777-7811
Extensive range of hardware fittings and accessories

Domus Housewares
85 Murray Street
Ottawa
Ontario. K1N 5M5
Tel: 613-241-6410
Fanciful and functional items for your
kitchen and home

Jaeggers
22 Third Avenue
Long Branch. NJ 07740
Tel: 908-870-2516
Wide range of pulls, knobs, and handles

Kraft
306 East 61st Street
New York. NY 10021
Tel: 212-838-2214
Hardware supplier, mail order service

Smith Woodworks & Design
101 Farmersville Road
Califon. NJ 07830
Tel: 908-832-2723
Carved and decorative knobs, pulls, switchcovers

Turnstyle Designs
Old World Joinery
8005 Roswell Road North East
Suite 130C
Atlanta. GA 30350
Tel: 770-518-1280
Contemporary shaped knobs, pulls, and accessories in
natural and metallic finishes

Useful Addresses

American Institute of Architects (AIA)
1735 New York Ave N.W.
Washington. DC 20006
Tel: 202-626-7300
Information on how to choose and work
with your architect

American Lighting Association
World Trade Center
2050 Stemmons Freeway
P.O. Box 530168
Dallas. TX 75258
Tel: 800-274-4484
Information on lighting products and
lighting manufacturers

Kitchen & Bath Source Book (annual)
MBC Data Distribution Publications
3901 West 86th Street, Suite 330
Indianapolis. IN 46268
Tel: 317-875-7776
Comprehensive guide to product design
and availability

Kitchen Cabinet Manufacturers Association
1899 Preston White Drive
Reston. VA 22091
Tel: 703-263-1690
Directory of member manufacturers

National Association of Plumbing, Heating & Cooling Contractors
Education Foundation
P.O. Box 6808
Falls Church. VA 22040-1148
Tel: 800-533-7694
For member referral

National Kitchen & Bath Association (NKBA)
687 Willowgrove Street
Hackettstown. NJ 07840
Tel: 800-367-6522
For member referral

Universal Design for Special Needs
Easy Access Housing
The National Easter Seal Society
70 East Lake Street
Chicago. IL 60601
Tel: 312-726-6200
Advice on improving home access

Index

Acknowledgments

The publishers would like to thank the following UK photographers and organizations for their kind permission to reproduce the photographs in this book. The page reference numbers are shown in bold type and the photographer or organization that supplied each picture is listed below.

Copyright holders are credited below where known. While every effort has been made to trace the copyright holders, we apologize for any omission and would be pleased to insert them in later editions.

1 Waring
2 Bulthaup UK Ltd.
4 Photography by Colin Walton.

Introduction
6–7 1 Fourneaux de France, **2, 3, 6** Bulthaup UK Ltd, **4** Plain & Simple Kitchens, **5** Fulham Kitchens.

Kitchen styles
15 Plain English Design Ltd, photography by Matthew Ward.
16 1 Bulthaup UK Ltd, **2** Keith Gray & Co, **3** Poggenpohl.
18, 20, 22, 24, 26, 28, 30, 32 Plain English Design Ltd, photography by Matthew Ward.
17, 19, 21, 23, 25, 27, 29, 31 Camargue plc and Blanco Ltd, photography by Matthew Ward.

Kitchen planning
33 Bulthaup UK Ltd.
34–35 1 Fucini by Miki Astori at Viaduct, **2** Bisque Ltd, **3** Kadfloor flooring from Kiani, **4** Roundhouse Design.
36–37 1 Dulux Paints, **2** Plain & Simple Kitchens, **3, 5, 7** Bulthaup UK Ltd, **4** Boffi Kitchens, **6, 10** SieMatic (CKP) Ltd, **8** Keith Gray & Co, **9** Plain & Simple Kitchens.
38–39 1, 6, 7, 11 Bulthaup UK Ltd, **2** Sub-Zero, **3** Sofiseb UK, **4, 10** SieMatic (CKP) Ltd, **5** Keith Gray & Co, **8** Woodstock Furniture, **9** Crabtree Kitchens.
40–41 1 Smallbone of Devizes, **2** Photography by James Merrell, **3** Chalon UK Ltd, **4** Bulthaup UK Ltd.

42–43 1, 2 Photography by Simon Upton, **4** Fulham Kitchens, **5** The Amtico Company Ltd, **6** Photography by Stephen Ward.
44–45 1, 2, 6 Crabtree Kitchens, **4** Dulux Paints, **5** Boffi Kitchens.
46–47 1, 5 Boffi Kitchens, **2** Bulthaup UK Ltd, **4** Mowlem & Co.
48–49 1, 6 Mowlem & Co, **2** Bulthaup UK Ltd, **4** Crabtree Kitchens, **5** Boffi Kitchens.
50–51 1, 5 Keith Gray & Co, **2** Fulham Kitchens, **4** Plain & Simple Kitchens, **6** Mitchell Beazley, **7** Bulthaup UK Ltd.
52 1 Photography by Simon Upton, **2** Woodstock Furniture, **3** Bulthaup UK Ltd, **4** Arc Linea.
53 Bulthaup UK Ltd.

Activity areas
54–55 1 Boffi Kitchens, **2** Keith Gray & Co, **3, 4** Bulthaup UK Ltd, **5** Crabtree Kitchens, **6** Sub-Zero.
56–57 1 Bulthaup UK Ltd, **2** Crabtree Kitchens, **3** Sub-Zero, **4** Roundhouse Design, **5** SieMatic (CKP) Ltd, **6** Keith Gray & Co.
58–59 1 Crabtree Kitchens, **2** SieMatic (CKP) Ltd, **3** Bulthaup UK Ltd, **4** Boffi Kitchens.
60–61 1 Fulham Kitchens, **2, 3** Bulthaup UK Ltd.
62–63 1 Bulthaup UK Ltd, **2, 4** Arc Linea, **3** Fulham Kitchens.
64–65 1 photography by Steve Tanner, **2** Crabtree Kitchens, **3** General Electric, **4** Chalon UK Ltd, **5** Neff UK Ltd, **6** Jenn-Air, **7** Plain & Simple Kitchens.
66–67 1 Photography by Simon Upton, **2** Fulham Kitchens, **3** Mitchell Beazley **4** Chalon UK Ltd, **5** SieMatic (CKP) Ltd, **6** Boffi Kitchens, **7** Romsey Cabinetmakers.
68 1 Neff (UK) Ltd, **2** SieMatic (CKP) Ltd.

Equipment
69 Fourneaux de France.
70–71 1 Fourneaux de France, **2** Bulthaup UK Ltd, **3** Siemens Domestic Appliances Ltd, **4** Roundhouse Design, **5** Divertimenti, **6** Kitchenmaid, **7** Gaggenau (UK) Ltd.
72–73 1 Ariston, **2** Viking, **3, 4** General Electric, **5** Imperial UK, **6** Aga, **7** Viking, **8** Smeg (UK) Ltd.
74–75 1 Poggenpohl, **2** Bosch, **3** Bulthaup UK Ltd, **4** Imperial UK, **5** Jenn-Air, **6, 7, 8, 9, 10** Miele Co. Ltd, **11, 12,** Ariston, **13** General Electric.
76–77 1, 6 Viking, **2** Zanussi Ltd, **3** Smeg (UK) Ltd, **4, 8** General Electric, **5** Neff (UK) Ltd, **7** Sub-Zero.
78–79 1 Crabtree Kitchens, **2** Keith Gray & Co, **3** Leisure, **4** Smeg (UK) Ltd, **5** Aero, **6, 8** Bulthaup UK Ltd, **7** Sub-Zero.
80 1, 2 Bosch, **3** Viking, **4** Miele Co. Ltd,.
81 1, 4 Whirlpool (UK) Ltd, **2** Ariston, **3** Admiral.
82 1, 5 Bulthaup UK Ltd, **2** Chalon UK Ltd, **3** Authentics, **4** General Electric.

Surfaces & finishes
83 Bulthaup UK Ltd.
84–85 1 Elon, **2** Bosch, **3** Junckers Ltd, **4, 5** Crown Berger Europe Ltd, **6** Crabtree Kitchens, **7** Chalon UK Ltd.
86–87 1 Photography by Simon Upton, **2, 5** Bulthaup UK Ltd, **3, 4** Arc Linea, **6** Plain & Simple Kitchens, **7** Neff (UK) Ltd, **8** Boffi Kitchens, **9** Crabtree Kitchens.
88–89 1 Crabtree Kitchens, **2** Chalon UK Ltd, **3, 5** John Cullen Lighting, **4** Bulthaup UK Ltd, **6** SieMatic (CKP) Ltd, **7** Design 4, **8** Uno Design System.
90–91 1 Paris Ceramics, **2** Dalsouple, photography by Colin Walton, **3** Bosch, **4** Mitchell Beazley, **5** The Amtico Company Ltd, **6** Junckers Ltd, **7** Mitchell Beazley.
92–93 1, 6 Fulham Kitchens, **2** Junckers Ltd,

3, 5 Keith Gray & Co, **4** Corian®, **7** GEC Anderson, **8** Plain & Simple Kitchens.
94–95 1 Bulthaup UK Ltd, **2** Neff (UK) Ltd, **3** Viaduct, **4, 7** Plain & Simple Kitchens, **5** Crown Berger Europe Ltd, **6** Photography by Simon Upton.
96 1 Smallbone of Devizes, **2** Chalon UK Ltd, **3** Keith Gray & Co, **4** Plain English Design Ltd.

Quick fixes
97 Photography by Simon Upton
98–99 1 The Conran Shop, **2** SieMatic, **3, 6** Photography by James Merrell, **4** Designers Guild, **5** Newcastle Furniture Company.
100–101 1 Keith Gray & Co, **2** The Shaker Shop, **3, 5, 6** Photography by Simon Upton, **4** John Lewis, **7** Fulham Kitchens, **8** Pinewood Designs, **9** Photography by James Merrell.
102–103 1 Leisure, **2, 3** Designers Guild, **4** Bosch, **5** Photography by Andrew Twort, **6** Plain & Simple Kitchens.
104–105 1 The Conran Shop, **2, 3, 11** Photography by Simon Upton, **4** The Holding Company, **5** Nazanin Kamali for Aero, **6, 7, 8, 9** Divertimenti, **10** Photography by Andrew Twort.

Illustrations
Colour illustrations by Richard Lee.
Line illustrations by Colin Walton.

Thanks to...
The author would like to thank the many companies who provided material for this book. Jerry and Margery; the US research team. Alex Myers for picture research and Matthew Ward for his photography. Walton and Pringle for their design and editorial skills. Finally, to Nelson and Angela who allowed me uninterrupted hours of writing.

Walton and Pringle would like to extend our thanks to Katie Fontana at Plain English Design Ltd and Russell Smith at Carmargue plc for their kitchens. Karmer Setbuilding for their construction skills and Matthew Ward for his photography. Blanco Ltd for loan of their sink and tap. Celia Warbrick for her advice. Furniture 151, and The Shaker Shop, for kitchen accessories. Dalsouple for their rubber flooring.